CREATING A CULTURE
OF MINDFUL INNOVATION
IN HIGHER EDUCATION

CREATING A CULTURE
OF MINDFUL INNOVATION
IN HIGHER EDUCATION

MICHAEL LANFORD
AND WILLIAM G. TIERNEY

Published by State University of New York Press, Albany

For information, contact State University of New York Press, Albany, NY
www.sunypress.edu

Library of Congress Cataloging-in-Publication Data

Names: Lanford, Michael, author. | Tierney, William G., author.
Title: Creating a culture of mindful innovation in higher education / Michael Lanford
    and William G. Tierney.
Description: Albany : State University of New York Press, [2022] | Includes
    bibliographical references and index.
Identifiers: ISBN 9781438487632 (hardcover : alk. paper) | ISBN 9781438487649
    (ebook) | ISBN 9781438487625 (pbk. : alk. paper)
Further information is available at the Library of Congress.

10 9 8 7 6 5 4 3 2 1

Contents

Chapter 1

An Introduction to Mindful Innovation in Higher Education

As the newly hired Chair of Institutional Support and Effectiveness at Valley State College, Nathan's passion was described as "infectious" by his colleagues. When discussing one of his favorite topics, such as the untapped potential of predictive analytics in education, Nathan could stop abruptly in mid-sentence, pull out his tablet, and call up any number of statistical tables and graphs to solicit your spontaneous opinion. "Look at this—we used to know so little about the lives of our students. But now we have a consistent stream of data about their performance over the first six weeks of the semester. Isn't this amazing? And we're just at the tip of the iceberg here!" Staff who worked in Nathan's department said there "was a new excitement" and that ever since he arrived "change was possible." One staff member shared that "I was so used to thinking that my work had little meaning or impact. Now that Nathan has arrived, I feel there's real purpose to what I do."

The President of Valley State College was happy about the publicity Nathan generated: "It's an honor for us to have a real innovator on campus," he professed during one Board of Trustees meeting. "But I don't know how long we'll be lucky enough to keep him here. I just hope we'll start to see the impact of his initiatives before he gets snatched up by someone else with more money."

After one administrative meeting, the president huddled with a couple of Board members who were well-known entrepreneurs in the community. He glanced across the room at a small group of English professors who had attended the meeting to voice their objections to changes in the college's medical plan. With a furtive gesture, he added:

> Like over there—we desperately need new ideas in the English department. I beg them to take on a bigger share of our online course offerings. I plead with them to meet with Nathan. He has fantastic tools they could use to make the first-year classes more effective and exciting to the students. They just won't do it, though. We're really missing an opportunity while Nathan is here.

~

The head of Valley State's English department was Charlotte, a well-regarded veteran who had taught at the college for over 25 years and served as section chair for nearly 15. The walls of her office had not seen sunlight in nearly as many years, as they were concealed by floor-to-ceiling bookshelves crammed with texts, folders, and monographs on Shelley, Byron, and other Romantic poets. Charlotte's desk was piled high with stacks of papers. They included retention data for all 86 sections of the college's first semester writing class; requisition forms for a new office chair; the contracts for Valley State's stable of 15 or so adjunct faculty members; and dozens of applications for a recent faculty job advertisement.

The framed certificate associated with a teaching award often served as a paperweight for an endless stream of student papers, the output of three classes Charlotte taught in the fall and spring sessions. Her duties as department head allowed for a relief of two classes each semester. From Monday through Thursday, Charlotte could usually be found in her office from 7:30 a.m. until 8 or 9 p.m. On Friday, she left "early"—at 4:30 p.m.—to spend weekends with her new granddaughter whose family lived 2 hours away by car.

In comparison to Nathan's bold vision for Valley State—which includes Chromebooks in every classroom and an online portal modeled after Khan Academy that will allow universal access to professors' lectures—Charlotte expresses a more modest goal for her department: "I would just like to provide a full position with health benefits to some of the adjuncts who have been working here for 10-plus years." She pulls out a sheet of paper from one of her desk drawers and invites a closer examination of its contents. "Look at this. It's an email from one of the writing instructors who has taught here longer than most of my full-timers. We have paid her

$2,500 a semester for each class she's taught for—I don't even remember how long—and she's apologizing to me that she can't teach here next year because she now has her middle school teaching credentials. We have let her down for years by not offering her a permanent position, and now she's worried about letting *me* down!"

Charlotte's eyes twinkle at the suggestion that online coursework, similar to that proposed by Nathan, might alleviate some of the staffing problems in her department. "Yes, I hear that all the time from the administration," she acknowledges. And then continues:

> They really want us to have larger sections—"innovate, scale"—I hear it all the time. But you have to understand, my under-standing of teaching, and especially the scholarship associated with that, has been accumulated on the job. Real, substantive feedback is not easily scaled. Plus, there are new challenges every year because the students aren't the same. Real students pay real money to go here. Something like half of our students live in poverty. A lot of them don't have computers at home. I don't lecture anymore because I'm responding to students' needs, and neither do most of my colleagues.

Notably absent from Charlotte's desk is a computer. It is sequestered to a corner of the room where Charlotte can keep an eye on the stream of emails that accumulate in her Outlook folder. When they reach "critical mass," she slides her chair over and answers them as quickly as possible, eschewing formal salutations and grammatical conventions.

Charlotte flashes a smile and adds, "They probably think I'm a hopeless Luddite. Maybe they're right."

Innovation: Necessary Consequence or Overused Buzzword?

If Nathan and Charlotte appear to be polar opposites in terms of personal-ity, interest in technology, and overall approaches to education, then good, because that is our intent. Many discussions about innovation in higher education have become polarized between those who agitate for rapid change and those who contend that a more measured response to education's contemporary problems is obligatory. For some, innovation is a necessary consequence of a competitive, globalized environment where educational institutions are engaged in a zero-sum game for resources, faculty talent, and measurable indicators of success. For others, innovation is perceived as little more than a buzzword in danger of being rendered meaningless due to overuse and a lack of critical interrogation about its appropriate place in educational discourse.

Over several years of research across the United States, from Florida to California, we have encountered many individuals like Nathan and Charlotte. They are similarly passionate about improving educational outcomes, especially for traditionally marginalized populations. They often make personal and financial sacrifices because they deeply believe in the mission statements of their respective institutions. They find real inspiration in the work of their immediate colleagues. And, when problems surface within their departments or programs, they are equally creative in how they draw upon personal expertise to develop ingenious, even innovative, solutions. Despite these many similarities, we are distressed to discover—time and time again—that very little discussion and negotiation occurs between the varied proponents and critics of innovation. The potential for innovation within institutions is all too often shortchanged, as well, by a lack of engagement with several organizational factors that can either promote or inhibit an innovative idea.

We believe that individuals like Nathan are not just promoters of technological progress and innovation. They are also guided by a vision to improve education that can, at times, be perceived as "too entrepreneurial," yet is grounded in the realities of a contemporary neoliberal environment that prizes the blending of financial and societal gain. We also believe that individuals like Charlotte are as innovative as Nathan. Their commitment to fundamental academic values, such as academic freedom, tenure, and an obligation to serving the public good, is not antithetical to innovative progress; rather, individuals like Charlotte can stimulate innovative activity and create the conditions for mindful innovation that we will outline in this book.

How Innovation Is Currently Perceived in Higher Education

An authoritative explanation of innovation in higher education has proven elusive, mainly because individual disciplines conceptualize innovation in markedly dissimilar ways. This lack of consensus about innovation need not be viewed as a weakness, however. One of the attractive qualities about "innovation" as a concept relates to its transferability and reconceptualization across different disciplinary areas, time periods, and cultures. Nevertheless, for innovation to have real meaning in higher education, it must have a well-defined conceptual field that acknowledges strengths, weaknesses, and challenges. Furthermore, a lexicon of interconnected terms should be defined in order for innovation to have meaning. For these reasons, in this book we will discuss how innovation relates to creativity, disruption, and entrepreneurship, among other associated terms.

Some contemporary books conflate the concept of innovation with technology, assuming that almost all technological progress will result in greater efficiency, better student outcomes, and data that can better inform policy (e.g., Lane, 2014; Wildavsky, Kelly, & Carey 2011). Others have followed the lead of Burton Clark (1998) in asserting that an entrepreneurial mindset must pervade the culture of the university if it is to thrive in the 21st century (e.g., Ferreira et al., 2018; Foss & Gibson, 2015; Gibb, Haskins, & Robertson, 2013; Hannon, 2013; Meissner, Erdil, & Chataway, 2018; Tiedemann, 2019). We assume a more measured stance that considers whether or not technology is well suited for specific educational environments, as well as the negative implications of premature disruption grounded in dubious philosophical justifications rather than empirical evidence. Additionally, we acknowledge that scholars need to consider the entrepreneurial impact of their work, but we also reaffirm the central importance of higher education's compact with society and underserved communities.

Business texts on innovation abound; accordingly, innovation in higher education has been defined, in no small part, by the writings of Harvard business professor and consultant Clayton Christensen. In particular, *The Innovative University: Changing the DNA of Higher Education from the Inside Out* by Christensen and Eyring (2011) has had an enduring influence on current thinking about innovation and higher education. Nonetheless, as we will discuss in detail throughout this book, Christensen's theory of disruption remains controversial, and his prediction that nearly half of all U.S. colleges and universities would be bankrupt or close to it has not materialized, even in the wake of the Covid-19 pandemic. Our text will not only offer insights into why disruption has been slow in higher education but also consider why different models of change may be preferable for many institutions.

At this point, it may obvious we are not "innovation boosters," believing everything new is to be embraced and everything old is to be viewed as outdated. We are, in fact, very concerned about the promulgation of facile rhetoric surrounding disruption and innovation that shortchanges a deeper understanding of the challenges higher education institutions face today. We are dismayed that an abundance of empirical literature about the organizational conditions which promote creativity and innovation has been overlooked in favor of simplistic, yet marketable, ideas about "disruption," "design," and "play" that are advanced by Silicon Valley scions with little interest or regard for the role universities can play in societal progress. We are further concerned that a tacit acceptance of neoliberal values and New Public Management (NPM) philosophies are shortchanging the role higher education can play in creating a more equitable society, developing innovations that can raise living standards, furthering scientific inquiry, and fostering democratic values.

Furthermore, some texts on innovation are not well grounded in the multidisciplinary literature necessary for a nuanced understanding of innovation. Rather, they are often "how to" cookbooks with limited appeal that frequently approach the topic from a single perspective (e.g., "online classes are the future") or offer top-down platitudes about the importance of strong leadership. Too much current literature on innovation lacks engagement with scholarly research that consistently demonstrates a positive relationship between innovation and the concepts of diversity, intrinsic motivation, autonomy, and creative conflict. A deeper understanding of how the concepts of time, efficiency, and trust impact innovation is needed. Additionally, we contend that four core pillars of academic life—academic freedom, tenure, shared governance, and institutional autonomy—are not impediments to innovation, nor are they a primary cause of higher education's financial woes, as some might claim (e.g., Vedder, 2019; Wetherbe, 2013). They are crucial protections for encouraging trial and error, fostering an organizational culture that respects expertise and welcomes critical perspectives, and stimulating creativity and innovation in the 21st-century university.

The primary goal of this book, then, is to offer a different vision for innovation in higher education. To wit, we begin by explaining why a deeper engagement with innovation is necessary; our argument is grounded in the notion that higher education occupies a central role as a catalyst for innovative ideas, products, and artistic and scientific development—and as a nurturer of human talent that can create and support innovation. We further suggest that higher education needs to remain central to discussions about innovation because a viewpoint that relegates innovation to the private sector is liable to reduce innovation to purely economic terms, exacerbate inequities for traditionally marginalized groups, and minimize the contributions that innovations can make for all of society. Afterward, we define the concept of innovation for higher education through a review of pertinent literature from the disciplines of business, psychology, sociology, and education, as well as the emergent field of innovation studies. We have three additional goals for this book. First, we identify the conditions that enable college and university administrators, as well as faculty, to promote a culture of what we shall define as mindful innovation in their institutions. Second, we mitigate irrational exuberance about innovation and instead offer a clear-headed analysis of its strengths and weaknesses, as well as the challenges in creating a culture of mindful innovation. Third, we make a case for our framework of mindful innovation as a more substantive and more pertinent vision for higher education than the rhetoric surrounding disruption and the prescriptive concepts advanced by neoliberal actors in today's higher education environment.

Why *Mindful* Innovation?

Similar to our conceptualization of "innovation," our use of "mindful innovation" is deliberate and requires a precursory explanation. "Mindfulness" has been subject to ubiquitous commodification in recent years, from mindful eating (promoted by Weight Watchers) to "mindful mints" (which is a candy that purports to reduce stress) (Gelles, 2019). As a result, mindfulness has evolved considerably from Buddhist roots that encourage the use of meditation and conscious "moment-to-moment" experiences as a way to relieve stress and establish clarity of vision (Kabat-Zinn, 2003). And like innovation, the idea of anything being "mindful" is perilously close to existing as an ambiguous Zen-like buzzword prized more for its presumed positive connotations rather than any specific meaning that can helpfully foster individual or institutional progress.

The construct of mindfulness, however, has also been attentively studied by psychologists interested in measuring, often through clinical interventions, how participation in mindful activities (such as social support groups or meditation) impacts individual change (Baer, 2003; Brown & Ryan, 2003), as well as physical health and cognitive performance (Crane, 2017; Creswell, 2017; Tang, Hölzel, & Posner, 2015). Shapiro and colleagues (2006) have formulated a "model of mindfulness" that is helpful to envision how we see "mindfulness" merging with innovation. The three axioms associated with mindful activities are "intention," "attention," and "attitude" (2006).

INTENTION

As defined by Kabat-Zinn (1994), intention is "enlightenment and compassion for all beings" (375), and is an essential state for understanding "why [one] is practicing in the first place" (32). We similarly believe that a focus on innovation requires two essential considerations relating to intention: (1) a concern grounded in social justice for how an innovative product or process impacts different groups of people, especially those who are traditionally marginalized, and (2) a robust institutional awareness for why the development and/or implementation of an innovation is necessary. It is not enough to innovate for innovation's sake, or for the pursuit of financial reward. Innovations in higher education should be useful to a targeted population and fill an identifiable, specific need in order to have positive, appreciable impact on individuals and society.

ATTENTION

Attention, in the context of mindfulness, pertains to the ways in which an individual consciously understands their own internal and external behaviors in a given moment. A couple of reliable arguments for innovation in today's higher education context is that "the world is moving at an increasingly rapid pace" or that "institutions need to keep pace with a globalized environment or else they will be left behind." While we appreciate the importance of decisive leadership—and the necessity of responding to global forces and external demands—we also believe that rapid administrative decision making without consultation from impacted actors within the organization undercuts a thorough consideration of three important dimensions of the innovation process. We will address these three dimensions—time, efficiency, and trust—in greater detail in our discussion of planning, developing, and implementing mindful innovation in Chapter 7. The main takeaway here is that no innovation stands a strong chance of adoption and diffusion unless the temporal and resource demands are well understood—and bonds of trust have formed through communication channels and consultation.

ATTITUDE

Attitude concerns "the qualities one brings to the act of paying attention" (376). It is one thing to assess the impact of an innovation in a cold, dispassionate fashion, relying on numerical data to ascertain the success (or failure) of an innovative process or product. However, we draw from empirical studies that demonstrate the collection and analysis of data must be multifaceted, relying also on qualitative feedback about how an innovation diffuses within a given group and has the potential to simultaneously merge with and alter aspects of the existing organizational culture.

As we will discuss in greater detail later, we base our understanding of mindfulness on these principles. Building from this base of understanding, we define mindful innovation through six central tenets: (1) societal impact; (2) the necessity of failure; (3) creativity through diversity; (4) respect for autonomy and expertise; (5) the consideration of time, efficiency, and trust; and (6) the incentivization of intrinsic motivation and progress over scare tactics and disruption.

In longer form, we contend that a mindful approach to innovation has the following tenets:

1. A focus on the *societal impact*, as well as the entrepreneurial potential, of any potential innovation, especially for traditionally marginalized groups.

2. A welcoming environment for experimentation that critically examines *failure* as a part of the innovation process.

3. The promotion of *creativity through diversity* by bringing together groups that represent a broad and diverse spectrum of experiences, backgrounds, and content areas.

4. A safeguarding of individual *autonomy* and respect for *expertise* through venerable institutional and personal protections, such as academic freedom, shared governance, tenure, and institutional independence.

5. A thorough and rigorous consideration of the dimensions of *time*, *efficiency*, and *trust*—and their impact on the adoption, development, and implementation of any innovation.

6. Incentives that simulate the *intrinsic motivation* of individuals and organizations invested in innovative *progress* rather than the promulgation of scare tactics that warn of impending disruption.

Outline of Chapters

With these tenets introduced, our book is organized in the following manner:

In Chapter 2, we appeal for a multifaceted conceptualization of innovation to do justice to higher education's unique status as an instrument for workforce development, community engagement, and cultural and scientific progress. To stimulate our discussion, we expand on the reasons why a more comprehensive understanding of innovation is necessary for contemporary higher education. First, knowledge-intensive industries and services have become vital to economic development in the 21st century (Manyika et al., 2013). Second, the astonishing development of technological and computerized systems threatens to undercut job sectors relating to transportation, logistics, support, production, construction, and service (Frey & Osborne, 2017).

Due to both of these factors, higher education needs to play a central role in developing creative and social intelligence skills in both younger and returning older students so that they might have viable talents for future labor markets. Therefore, many national higher education sectors across the globe, particularly in developing countries, may engage in deliberate massification strategies that reflect these changing workforce demands. At the very least, a period of dynamic change concerning enrollment patterns is likely on the horizon. These strategies will be challenging to develop and implement, however, as the Covid-19 pandemic has engendered substantial uncertainty about the future of colleges and universities around the world. In addition, government funding for higher education in many nations is being cut, especially in Europe and North America, even while educational quality remains a priority and institutional change seems inevitable.

In Chapter 3, we first explore whether or not higher education is in "deep crisis," as Peter Drucker once famously remarked, by reviewing three signs of what we call a "fractured system": (1) explosive levels of student debt; (2) concern about the public perception of higher education; and (3) demographic and institutional instabilities in the sector. We then undertake a selective review of how one might employ innovation theories to make sense of these problems. Central to this discussion is Joseph Schumpeter's classic writings on innovation in the 1920s and 1930s. Contrary to many modern thinkers, Schumpeter (1942/2003) emphasized the importance of time and the luxury of hindsight when distinguishing between a new product or process and a truly innovative one. His insights are also notable for their consideration of the potentially negative aspects of innovation, along with his famous admonition that innovation could unleash a "process of creative destruction" (p. 83) by creating markets for new technologies (like oil and steel) that could transfigure entire economic sectors and cause social upheaval. A consideration of Schumpeter's writings sheds light on today's discourse on innovation, with its emphasis on the necessity for continuous innovation to maintain a competitive advantage in a hypercompetitive marketplace.

We then compare these early 20th-century writings with contemporary theorists, such as Clayton Christensen (1997), who have often embraced Schumpeter's rhetoric when considering the interplay between innovation and institutional survival. The influence of Christensen's "theory of disruptive innovation" for higher education is highlighted, given its frequent citation by administrators and policymakers interested in arguing for change and reform in today's colleges and universities. As theorized by Christensen, a disruptive innovation initially serves the bottom of a given market and has four distinguishing characteristics from its competitors: (1) simplicity, (2) affordability, (3) convenience, and (4) the ability to provide a product or service to nonconsumers who lack an alternative. For these reasons, for-profit colleges and universities, as well as Massive Open Online Courses (MOOCs), have been proposed as forces that would disrupt higher education, improve efficiency, and expand opportunity, if they were given enough time and resources. Although we acknowledge the power of Christensen's theory, particularly from rhetorical and visionary perspectives, we express deep concerns about the ideological imprint of disruptive innovation on higher education, as well as the lack of empirical evidence for its theoretical claims. Hence, we conclude that while the crises facing higher education are valid and require substantive change, they do not necessarily rise to the level where "disruption" to the entire sector is necessary or wise. Instead, we propose that other models of innovation based on a more careful deliberation of existing problems, a marshalling of the tremendous intellectual and creative resources of colleges and universities, and a focus on solutions that help marginalized individuals as much as they help elite actors—as modeled by "responsible innovation" in Europe—should be embraced.

Chapter 4 critically considers the manner in which higher education's problems, as outlined in Chapter 3, have been analyzed. Drawing on empirical data and research, we take issue with the claim that tenure is the source of multiple problems in higher education—from the rising cost of tuition to the stagnation of new pedagogical approaches. We demonstrate that the discourse concerning tenure has distracted observers of higher education from noticing three developments that have been, at least in part, influenced by neoliberal philosophies and the administrative principles behind New Public Management: (1) the growth in administrative size and salaries; (2) the outsourcing of important institutional activities; and (3) a lack of appreciation for the benefits that job protections provide to innovative inquiry. We then point out two cultural outcomes related to NPM's attack on tenure. First, an institutional culture conductive to creative and innovative exploration is harmed, not helped, by the erosion of tenure. Second, education is reduced to a commodity that is traded on the market, rather than as a public good that is intended to benefit individuals and society through shared access. Therefore, while we acknowledge the importance of efficiency and effectiveness as important dimensions for any organization to consider, we contend that they can assume outsized importance in an environment attempting to implement the strategies of NPM while fostering an innovative culture. We conclude the chapter with an admonition that the flaws of neoliberalism prevent us from effectively cultivating an innovative environment and, in turn, resolving the many pressing and immediate problems that higher education faces.

In Chapters 5 through 7, we extend our previous writings on innovation published by the TIAA Institute and the *Higher Education Handbook of Theory and Research*[1] to develop, in this book, a new conceptual model of *Mindful Innovation in Higher Education*. We begin in Chapter 5 with a consideration of how "innovation," along with related concepts such as "creativity" and "entrepreneurship," remains underconceptualized and little understood, particularly with regards to higher education. Too often, in higher education and the business world, new ideas and/or processes are labeled as "innovative" before individuals have an opportunity to understand their full impact. As discussed in our narrative with Nathan and Charlotte, the relentless association of "innovation" with "positive development" has caused many within higher education to dismiss the concept as a hollow marketing term with little useful meaning. We will suggest, however, that both a nuanced understanding of innovation as a concept and critical engagement with the term are necessary if individuals and institutions are to consider it in a valuable manner.

We first draw from the humanities to cite several examples of how innovation has been viewed in cinema, literature, and music. We also draw on these examples to discuss how individual endeavor and creativity can result in innovative ideas. By considering how innovation is viewed when a profit motive is not at the forefront, we make important distinctions between "creativity," "innovation," and "entrepreneurship" and formulate definitions that resonate with the complex missions of colleges and universities.

Creativity refers to inventiveness grounded in field-specific knowledge and expedited by motivation. Even though people assume novelty is equated with creativity, it is not a necessary condition to be creative. Instead, we demonstrate how novelty, assessed through the perspective of hindsight, is intricately related to innovation. Implementation is necessary for a product or process to undergo diffusion, an essential step in assessing an innovation's societal impact (Rogers, 2003). Thus, innovation pertains to the implementation of a creative product or process and its perceived novelty and impact within a given field once it has undergone diffusion and evaluation by a critical audience. While creativity is a necessary condition for innovative thinking, not all creative individuals or organizations have been innovative. Examples of potentially innovative ideas that were not fully implemented (or took decades to recognize) will help the reader understand the complex relationship between creativity and innovation, as well as the ways in which institutional definitions of "success" can impact diffusion.

Meanwhile, innovations, as described by Mars and Rios-Aguilar (2010), can serve as "catalysts for entrepreneurial activities" (454) that are focused on capital gain. Entrepreneurship is thus defined as a creative organizational activity and/or process reliant upon innovation but primarily motivated by the potential for this capital gain. We interrogate the relationship of creativity and entrepreneurship with innovation to demonstrate how they are interconnected on individual and organizational levels, as well as to demarcate differences.

Chapters 6 and 7 present the central ideas necessary to operationalize mindful innovation. In Chapter 6, we employ existing scholarship to identify four environmental factors—diversity, intrinsic motivation, autonomy, and creative conflict—that stimulate innovation in organizational cultures. Numerous studies indicate that organizations utilizing a diverse group of individuals are more innovative. Diversity is defined here by a variety of attributes, such as an individual's areas of expertise, multiplex and intersecting identities, and cultural knowledge. Studies show that a diverse leadership enables employees to propose novel concepts and understand the perspectives of a more diverse range of clients. Furthermore, leaders are more likely to expedite feedback channels, ensure that multiple voices are heard, and delegate authority. Each of these behaviors help both leadership and employees fulfill their innovative potential to a greater degree than they would in a less diverse environment.

Research by psychologists conclusively demonstrates that tapping into an individual's intrinsic motivation is a more effective avenue than extrinsic motivation to stimulate creative and innovative thinking. Unfortunately, it has become increasingly common for leaders, even in higher education, to use financial incentives (as a form of extrinsic motivation) to reward desired behavior and direct resources toward predetermined goals. Throughout this book, we cite documented examples of instances in which financial rewards, especially during the invention and implementation stages, have encouraged shortcuts that failed to produce truly novel, or innovative, thinking.

Related to incentives is the issue of autonomy. One trend that threatens to inhibit innovation in higher education is the increasing prevalence of evaluative processes excessively focused on externally derived measures of assessment (Amabile et al., 1996). To nurture an innovative climate in colleges and universities, we maintain that a certain degree of autonomy is necessary. This is especially important for highly motivated individuals who often choose a life in higher education so they might enjoy greater autonomy than they would have in other work sectors. Finally, we demonstrate how higher education has started to eschew constructive critique in favor of "collegiality." This trend has led to an attitude among administrators that anyone who opposes their worldview—and the policies that spring from it—is not a part of the "team" and needs to be pushed aside in order for progress and disruption to occur. We argue vehemently against this notion, asserting that "group-think" results in unfavorable conditions for the incubation of creativity and innovation. Instead, higher education needs to foster constructive critique so that diverse individuals, particularly those who might be marginalized, can voice their perspectives and expertise, and the institutional conditions for mindful innovation can ultimately be cultivated.

In Chapter 7, we focus on three dimensions—time, efficiency, and trust—that directly impact an organization's ability to plan, develop, and implement an innovation. Time is intricately correlated with the implementation process, and subject to a complex array of considerations unique to each innovative project. The predominantly negative, and occasionally positive, effects of efficiency on innovation are explored. Elements of an institution's social structure will be outlined with reference to concrete examples from our own research. Moreover, we argue that trust has to be engendered by an environment that allows for an open discussion of ideas, even when opinions diverge. As such, we shall argue that an innovative institution needs to carefully consider how to manage the temporal aspects of an innovative process, balance the demands for efficiency with the need to adequately supply innovative institutions and researchers, and generate the conditions for trust so that resources are allocated appropriately and innovative inquiry can transpire.

Much of the decision making in higher education occurs at the institutional level. Therefore, we also expand on the three aforementioned dimensions of innovation to delineate how institutional decision makers can plan the adoption and implementation of a "foreign" innovation. From a mindful perspective, an innovation should be carefully considered in three ways: (1) its institutional fit, (2) its potential impact, and (3) its likely longevity. Without a comprehensive examination of these factors, our own experience with institutional adoption and implementation indicates that even the most promising of innovations are likely to have minimal impact due to the prevailing cultural norms of the organization.

Building on the historical, conceptual, and empirical discussions of innovation in the preceding chapters, Chapter 8 begins as a cautionary tale about the shortcomings of current rhetoric on innovation. American higher education came of age in the 20th century. If international rankings existed in the 19th century, no more than a handful of American colleges or universities would have been considered "world class." Today, more than half of the world's best institutions on every league table are located in the United States. Therefore, a conundrum exists. On the one hand, America's postsecondary institutions are viewed as moribund. Yet, on the other, they are thought of as the world's best. A propensity of Nobel Prize awards has gone to scientists who conduct research in the United States. The American professorate is more cited than faculty in any other country, and by every innovative measure—patents, intellectual property, start-ups, and the like—America's colleges and universities have been leading exemplars.

How is it possible that American higher education can be in dire need of innovation when, by virtually every available method of analysis, America's postsecondary institutions are doing better than any other institution or system? We answer these questions by arguing that four traditional, yet important, tenets of American higher education—academic freedom, tenure, shared governance, and institutional autonomy—remain indispensable for fostering a creative intellectual environment that can result in innovative progress.

Chapter 9 ties our arguments together and reaffirms our primary arguments about the need for mindful innovation in higher education. The 21st-century university is one that shall remain wedded to core concepts, such as academic freedom, while at the same time adapting to environmental constraints and evolving to meet societal concerns. During a great period of U.S. higher education expansion in the late 19th and early 20th centuries, colleges and universities adapted and evolved; in doing so, they seized strategic opportunities that enabled innovative thinking while European institutions lagged behind. We shall review the conditions that afford similar opportunities to postsecondary institutions throughout the world in the 21st century.

We shall, however, offer three cautions. First, although the tenor of this book is not that of a doomsayer, we shall suggest that administrators and faculty unwilling to consider the parameters of environmental change are likely to put their institutions at long-term risk. We particularly focus here on colleges caught in the throes of enrollment declines and states unwilling to adequately fund higher education or regulate the for-profit industry. Both examples highlight the challenges of innovation from different perspectives.

The second caution relates to those individuals whom Rogers (2003), in his work on the diffusion of innovations, defines as "early adopters," such as those who have embraced virtual learning. We caution that unfounded exuberance runs the risk not only of failing to meet expectations but also of lessening the climate for innovation. As we will have discussed in earlier chapters, innovation is not a series of organizational revolutions, nor is it a structure that is in constant flux. Paradoxically, innovation is planned, and spaces for innovative thinking are strategically built into the organization.

Finally, we shall suggest that the university of the future will still likely be place-bound and populated by faculty who largely define their work as teaching students and conducting research. The culture in which they undertake these activities, however, will be dramatically different from that of today. The institutions that can socialize their participants to an innovative culture are likely to be the ones that will appear in the league tables of tomorrow and be hailed for their significant contributions not only to labor markets and entrepreneurial endeavors but also to greater social equity and scientific progress.

Chapter 2

Understanding the Need for
Mindful Innovation in Higher Education

In a world where scientific breakthroughs and new technological gadgets frequently grab headlines and capture the imagination of the general public, every institution wants to be recognized as "innovative." *Forbes*, *FastCompany*, and *Fortune* each annually publish rankings of the "most innovative" companies. Not to be outdone, *U.S. News & World Report* recently started publishing an annual ranking of the "most innovative schools." The potential for long-term economic growth is often linked with a region's innovative activity (Rosenberg, 2004). From fields as diverse as the armed forces (Fastabend & Simpson, 2004) to the legal profession (Mazzone, 2013), the motto "adapt or die" has been embraced as a mantra that promotes transformative change through innovation. Many even assert that a culture of innovation is necessary for survival, lest a rival seize a competitive advantage in the marketplace of ideas, making its erstwhile peers obsolete. Consequently, the inevitability of innovative progress is reinforced on a daily basis.

Higher education has not been immune to this escalating global interest in innovation. As public higher education institutions around the world continue to suffer from decreased state funding, institutions are seeking new ways to increase revenue through entrepreneurial ventures that emphasize innovative research and teaching (Daniels & Spector, 2016; Marginson, 2013; Slaughter & Rhoades, 2004; Toma, 2011). Small private colleges that lack large endowments seek to be innovative and develop turnaround strategies that will prevent their collapse, particularly in the face of changing demographics that could negatively impact student enrollment over the next few years (Grawe, 2018, 2021). Innovative pedagogical methods and modes of delivery are likely required to match the dynamic interplay between workforce development and higher education, especially in developing countries (Goddard, 2012). Moreover, government demands for greater efficiency in national higher education sectors have compelled a desire for innovative institutional structures and organizations (Powell, Gilleland, & Pearson, 2012). These demands are sure to grow in the wake of the Covid-19 pandemic. The same entrepreneurial spirit has led to the establishment of education hubs in various countries throughout the world. Ministries of education in these countries hope that university-led research and development might stimulate the next Silicon Valley or Oxbridge (Knight, 2011; Olds, 2007), and many for-profit higher education institutions have been praised for tapping into an innovation ideology.

In short, higher education is currently confronted by global forces that necessitate innovative research, innovative pedagogies, innovative partnerships, and innovative organizational structures. While some may consider these changes a threat to traditional academic life, innovative research can provide immeasurable benefits to society in the form of medical and technological breakthroughs, inventions that improve global sustainability, and interdisciplinary ventures that raise the quality of life for millions, particularly in poverty-stricken regions (Khavul & Bruton, 2012). For these reasons, we suggest in this chapter that a deeper conceptual understanding of innovation is critical for higher education's continued development—and, most importantly, its relevance to society—in the 21st century.

To support this notion, we first detail three societal conditions that have sharpened higher education's focus on innovation as a topic worthy of continued interrogation—and we will begin with a story about how one innovation had a prodigious effect on society.

Innovation—or Instrument of Destruction?

Now that we are more than 20 years into the 21st century, it is apparent that the underlying conditions of economic development have changed markedly from those at the turn of the century. But why have economic conditions changed so profoundly? And what are the effects? Depending on one's area of study and theoretical alignment, a multitude of global forces and their impact on markets and society could be martialed as evidence. Regardless, there is considerable agreement that an inflection point occurred in September 2007, when a global financial crisis threatened the financial stability of banks and, through association, stock markets and currencies throughout the world. The statistics remain startling today. Five years after the crisis began, the Treasury Department of the United States estimated the total country's loss of household wealth at $19.2 trillion. At its peak in October 2009, the unemployment rate reached double digits—at 10.1%. To prevent the further capitulation of financial institutions, the U.S. government distributed approximately $23 trillion in bailout money.[1] A recent study by the Federal Reserve Bank of San Francisco stated that the financial crisis cost each U.S. citizen approximately $70,000 in lifetime income (Barnichon, Matthes, & Ziegenbein, 2018).

A decline in innovation mirrored the deterioration of household wealth. Universities and companies had fewer resources to devote to research and development, a phenomenon revealed through statistical data concerning patent applications. From 1983 to 2007, U.S. patent applications rose at an unprecedented rate, with a dramatic increase from 2000 (164,795 applications) to 2007 (241,347 applications). In 2008, however, patent applications decreased to 231,588, and in 2009 they decreased even further, to 224,912.[2]

By this point in time, the causes and contagions of the 2007–2008 financial crisis have been well documented by journalists and scholars. Nevertheless, they are worth briefly reiterating, as they involve the "rhetoric" of innovation and the way in which it is occasionally associated with "positive change" in the fields of economics and business.

The seeds of the financial crisis can be attributed to the incremental, yet steady, deregulation of the banking industry from approximately 1980 to the first decade of the 20th century. Deregulation set the stage for two destructive activities to occur in tandem. The first activity concerned rapacious lending practices by banks interested in making the acquisition of credit as easy as possible. One of their most popular methods was to offer subprime loans to individuals who either had previous problems with debt or limited debt experience. These lending practices were facilitated by a drop in the required FICO score for "prime" borrowers from 660 (in the early 2000s) to 620 (by 2005). Many of the people who entered the subsequently lower "subprime" lending market were also likely victims of discrimination in the past, had low levels of financial literacy, and had very few substantive assets to offer as collateral against a potential default (Dunbar & Donald, 2009; Steil et al., 2018). A subset of predatory banks made it difficult, if not virtually impossible, for many of their borrowers to pay their bills by instituting "financial innovations" that required individuals without internet access to pay electronically, charging exploitative interest rates, and tacking on interminable fees (Frame & White, 2014). These innovations had the cumulative effect of causing delinquencies and defaults to rise sharply, especially among Black and Latinx populations and in fast-growing parts of the country such as Florida and Nevada (Mayer & Pence, 2008).

The second activity involved the emergence of "derivatives"—then also hailed as an "innovative" financial instrument" not only by free-market advocates for financial deregulation but also by a number of Keynesian economists who wield considerable influence on economic policy. Derivatives are complex securities that derive their value from underlying baskets of assets, such as mortgages, loans, and other various forms of debt. In 2000, then-President Bill Clinton effectively banned regulation of the derivatives market by signing the Commodities Futures Modernization Act. As a result, the derivatives market became extremely popular because it was seen as an "efficient" way to manage an assortment of financial risks, and, by June 2008, the total value of derivative contacts was estimated at $683 trillion.

Knowing what we know now—that the baskets of derivatives were heavily tainted by subprime loans impossible for banks to clear—it is somewhat difficult to recreate the heady days in which derivatives were seen as a magnificent innovation that could drastically improve markets. Hence, a speech given by Alan Greenspan, then Chairman of the U.S. Federal Reserve, on September 25, 2002, to the London Society of Business Economists helps us to understand the thinking of financial analysts and economic theorists at that time. Reading from remarks that would later be entitled "Regulation, Innovation, and Wealth Creation," Greenspan began by heralding the innovators of previous generations who made substantive contributions to science:

> Since the dawn of the Industrial Revolution here in Britain, virtually every generation in the industrialized world has witnessed advances in living standards. A never-ending stream of innovation has led inexorably to expanded trade and improved productivity in many nations throughout the world. . . . Our modern electronic devices work according to the laws of quantum mechanics, which were laid out in the 1920s by Erwin Schrodinger, Werner Heisenberg, and Paul Dirac . . . The major revolutions of Albert Einstein had occurred a few years earlier and nuclear power was a generation or so beyond.

I raise such examples only to emphasize that we cannot realistically project future innovations and the potential for those innovations to create economic value. Novel insights, by definition, have not previously entered anyone's consciousness. However, that unanticipated discoveries of how to create wealth will emerge in the decades ahead no longer seems as conjectural as it may have, for example, before the Industrial Revolution.

After briefly acknowledging that a "global financial system" could [increase] systemic risk," Greenspan extolled the benefits of a transparent market where "fully informed market participants" could "generate the most efficient allocation of capital." Then, he entertained the prospect of similar innovations making a positive societal impact by turning his attention to the "derivatives market" as an "innovation" that could "create economic value":

> An example more immediate to current regulatory concerns is the issue of regulation and disclosure in the over-the-counter derivatives market . . . But regulation is not only unnecessary in these markets, it is potentially damaging, because regulation presupposes disclosure, and forced disclosure of proprietary information can undercut innovations in financial markets . . .
>
> All participants in competitive markets seek innovations that yield above-normal returns. In generally efficient markets, few find such profits. But those that do exploit such discoveries earn an abnormal return for doing so. In the process, they improve market efficiency by providing services not previously available.[3]

The takeaways from this retelling of the 2007 financial crisis are twofold. First, not all "innovations" have a universally positive impact on society. In fact, the majority of innovations have a range of effects, impacting diverse individuals, communities, and institutions in markedly dissimilar ways. Initially, the positive impacts an innovation can have on society are often legally restricted by patents, a governmental concern about unintended consequences, or the need for comprehensive testing. While people may complain about such regulations as getting in the way of innovative progress, there are numerous examples, similar to the 2007 financial crisis, where an untested innovation resulted in disastrous consequences. Nevertheless, even after the 2007 financial crisis, many economists at prominent institutions and universities continued to complain that the innovative potential of derivatives would be unfairly constrained by regulations. For example, a team of economists at New York University wrote the following in 2009:

> The problems that arose were not associated with all derivatives, but primarily with over-the-counter (OTC) derivatives and, in particular, the newer credit derivative market. And, even then, the issue should not be with the derivatives as an instrument, but with (i) the way they were traded and cleared, and (ii) how they were used by some financial institutions to increase their exposure to certain asset classes.
>
> A considerable portion of financial innovation over the last 30 years has come from the emergence of derivative markets . . . Even in the current financial crisis, the derivative scapegoat, credit default swaps (CDS), has played some positive roles. (Acharya, et al., 2009)[4]

We do not argue with the notion that innovations have a positive role in every field of human endeavor. However, an innovation's capacity for positive change can be turned against society by the selfish, yet unfortunately rational, motives of a few individuals who seek to profit from the innovation's inherent complexity or its novelty. This is what happened with the innovation of "derivatives," and, as we shall see later in this book, other similarly undertested and underregulated innovations in recent years.

Second, this narrative serves to underscore the turbulence many fields within society, including higher education, experience as an increasingly globalized environment has increased the complexity of everyday life. Another innovation entered the marketplace with relatively little fanfare in 2007: the Apple iPhone. At the time, Apple was an established brand name in the field of personal computing but an interloper in the marketplace of cell phones, which was dominated by several established companies including BlackBerry, LG, Nokia, Motorola, Siemens, and Sony. A previous collaboration with Motorola to integrate Apple's iTunes environment in a cell phone had been a notorious failure. Steve Jobs wanted the Motorola collaboration, called the Rokr E1, to hold 1,000 songs; it could hold only approximately 100. The case was made from cheap plastic and housed a poor-quality camera. Even worse, during the choreographed product introduction of the iTunes environment on the Rokr phone, Steve Jobs hit the wrong button and failed to demonstrate the device's ability to resume music after a phone call.[5]

The iPhone, by contrast, was designed completely by Apple engineers and was a strange device—and a tremendous risk—for its time. It had only one button, it did not have the easily accessible and removable battery to which customers had become accustomed, and it compelled users to adjust to a completely novel touchscreen interface. The interface itself was potentially disconcerting, as the user had to navigate a series of icons and widgets representing different apps housed by the phone's internal storage. To unlock the phone, the user swiped across the screen, a feature inspired by the bathroom locks on an airplane (Merchant, 2017). Nevertheless, it was a massive success. It disrupted the industry of cell phone production and ushered in a new age of smartphones that unpredictably became the preferred internet access device for millions of users.

Devices like the iPhone have led people to look for other seemingly inert industrial and commercial sectors where novel ideas have been lacking for some time—or where an entrenched hierarchy appears to be stifling creativity. Colleges and universities, as a result, have come under scrutiny. Further, evolving economic conditions and technological advancements have heightened the need for higher education to prove its value to both society and the nation-state, as the next section will discuss.

Three Societal Conditions Challenging Traditional Roles within Higher Education

1. The "Knowledge Economy"

Colleges and universities around the world are responding to a dizzying array of internal and external stakeholder expectations (Jongbloed, Enders, & Salerno, 2008). Internal stakeholders, such as boards of trustees and influential alumni groups, frequently emphasize the importance of institutional prestige and competitiveness, as determined by accumulated wealth and research productivity measures that translate to improvement in global ranking systems (Tierney & Lanford, 2017). Meanwhile, external stakeholders, such as politicians and employers, demand amplified accountability through a variety of performance-oriented metrics (Hillman, Tandberg, & Fryar, 2015; Rutherford & Rabovsky, 2014). As a result, colleges and universities are devising innovative curricula to remediate the types of academic skills students need to succeed in college, reformulating degree curricula that translate directly into specific job sectors, and expanding student support programs in the hopes of increasing the proportion of students who graduate with postsecondary degrees (Dougherty, Lahr, & Morest, 2017; Page & Gehlbach, 2017). The convergence of these pressures is occurring during a time in which state investments in higher education, following neoliberal philosophies that extol institutional self-sufficiency, have been slashed on an annual basis in many countries throughout the world—and may face even greater disinvestment due to the Covid-19 pandemic (Estermann et al., 2020; Jackson & Saenz, 2021; Marginson, 2013; Mitchell et al., 2018; Muscio, Quaglione, & Vallanti, 2013; Oliff et al., 2013; Olssen, 2016).

A concurrent discourse has emerged about the need for higher education systems to support a "knowledge economy." Prior to 2008, two types of cross-border trade were vital to global economic development: (1) labor-intensive flows from nations with developing economies and (2) commodity-intensive flows from nations with developed economies (Manyika et al., 2013). The main drivers of globalization, however, have changed dramatically since the 2008 financial crisis. Today, knowledge-intensive services are indispensable to workforce development.

This knowledge economy is less dependent on industrial production, and more attentive to three other factors: (1) the cultivation of STEM-related knowledge among workers and researchers; (2) a willingness to collaborate with not only experts in different fields but also business and industry representatives; and (3) creative solutions to many of society's most vexing concerns, including the increasing divide between urban and rural societies and the persistence of socioeconomic inequities. Richard Florida (2013) has written extensively on this topic, highlighting the contemporary importance of creativity and innovation while arguing that this shift "represents an epochal transition" for people around the world:

> Ever since the transition from feudalism to capitalism, the basic source of productivity, value, and economic growth has been physical labor and manual skill. In the knowledge-intensive organization, intelligence and intellectual labor replace physical labor as the fundamental source of value and profit (p. 232).

In summary, industries are expected to adapt quickly to the challenges of conducting business in a globalized marketplace, innovations in virtual communication that lower the costs of collaboration across borders, and the shifting competencies and skills required from workers as technology evolves.

As a result, those institutions that can identify and incorporate valuable innovations will likely have a substantial advantage over their competitors in the global marketplace. Within higher education, countries that can nurture innovative environments for research and inquiry will similarly have robust advantages, especially if they can stimulate development between universities and industry. The regions that can foster such a relationship will be recognized as "educational hubs," similar to those found in Silicon Valley in the United States, Singapore in Southeast Asia, or Oxbridge in the United Kingdom, and they will be well situated to flourish in the 21st-century knowledge economy (Castells, 2004; Knight, 2011; Knight & Morshidi, 2011; Lauder & Mayhew, 2020; Olds, 2007).

2. Envisioning the Workforce of the Future

Many countries are grappling with the pressures of globalization and the fluctuating labor demands of our contemporary knowledge economy. The most in-demand competencies for jobs of the future will be judgment and decision-making abilities, communication skills, analytical prowess, and administrative capabilities (Frey & Osborne, 2017). There is also a demonstrated need for workers proficient in technology and trained to think critically, especially with cultural understanding and awareness.

To cite the United States as an example, data indicate that the completion of a 4-year undergraduate degree not only facilitates greater lifetime income for individuals (Gould, 2017) but also improved societal outcomes relating to crime, health, and welfare reliance (Carnevale, Rose, & Cheah, 2013; Trostel, 2015). Moreover, researchers from Columbia University have demonstrated that attendance at 2-year institutions is correlated with significant private earning gains over the course of a lifetime (Belfield & Bailey, 2017). In short, the disparity has never been greater between individuals who hold some form of higher education credential and those who do not. As a result, politicians, policymakers, and researchers have consistently emphasized the need for improved degree completion rates in U.S. colleges and universities.

Yet according to the most recent census data from the United States, only 47% of the national population aged 25 years of age and older holds a postsecondary credential.[6] Due to decreased state funding for higher education, the cost of college has risen sharply in recent years while capacity has become strained in all but a handful of state colleges and universities. Students are increasingly compelled to juggle part-time and full-time employment, childcare, and other personal and family responsibilities while undertaking demanding course loads (Goldrick-Rab, 2016).

Why do so many students need access to higher education in the 21st century? Part of the answer resides in the changing economy and the types of jobs that will be available in the coming decades. The outsourcing of manufacturing and service jobs over the past 2 decades has been well chronicled (Bhagwati, Panagariya, & Srinivasan, 2004; Levine, 2011). Increasingly, however, awareness is growing that many job sectors once considered "stable"—such as transportation, logistics, support, and construction—are in the process of being weakened, or even thoroughly transformed, by the astonishing development of technological and computerized systems. This development is a continuation of the escalating pace of technological innovation that contributed mightily to wage polarization in the 1980s and 1990s (Autor, Katz, & Kearney, 2006) and will likely change the nature of work in other job sectors over the next few decades (Brynjolfsson & McAfee, 2011). In past years, computerization was limited by rule-based activities that facilitated impressive number-crunching but allowed only routine tasks to be accomplished. Today, as many as half of the jobs in the United States may be thoroughly transformed by improvements in processing power, algorithmic sophistication, sensors, and equipment controlled by computers (Frey & Osborne, 2017). "Nonroutine" cognitive tasks related to large sectors of employment—such as law enforcement (Petit, 2018; Rademacher, 2020), medical diagnosis (Marques, Agarwal, de la Torre Díez, 2020; Park & Han, 2018), the navigation of aerial and surface vehicles (Nakamura & Kajikawa, 2018; Stenquist, 2021), and writing in the fields of journalism (Graefe & Bohlken, 2020; Wölker & Powell, 2021) and law (Campbell, 2020; Wu, 2020) are therefore perceived as being increasingly viable options for computerization and automation.

The potential impacts of improvements to alternative forms of energy production, such as wind and solar, and the resulting negative impacts on legacy energy sectors, such as oil and natural gas, also remain to be seen. To cite just one example, Bloomberg NEF (2020) predicts that electric vehicles will constitute 28% of all global passenger vehicle sales by 2030 and 58% of all vehicle sales by 2040. While other major markets, such as the United States, may lag in the short term due to entrenched business interests, they will likely find it difficult to resist trends that impact global supply chains (Meckling & Hughes, 2018), innovations in the production of batteries and electrical storage (International Energy Agency, 2020), and widespread demand for newer technologies due to consumer preferences and environmental concerns (Hazboun & Boudet, 2020; Liao, Molin, & van Wee, 2017). As a result, workers who have significant experience and expertise in certain legacy industries may be displaced, unable to find secure reemployment in their given fields, and in need of substantial retraining to reenter a labor market that often lacks clarity in terms of employment prospects and viable opportunities for higher education that are both convenient and affordable (Das & Hilgenstock, 2018). Such trends are disquieting for those who already observe that job opportunities in labor markets throughout the world have become limited and wages have become hierarchically stratified, particularly on the basis of race, ethnicity, gender, and class (Arce & Segura, 2015; Autor & Dorn, 2013).

Additionally, job displacements provoked by the Covid-19 pandemic have encouraged both companies and governments to explore greater efficiency and new ways to incorporate virtual interaction in a variety of sectors (Hollander & Carr, 2020). The potential benefits and limitations of virtual teaching and learning were most widely apparent in 2020, as millions of primary, secondary, and tertiary students throughout the world were thrust into new learning environments (we discuss online learning in higher education in greater detail later in the book). Nevertheless, prominent economists who have studied the impact of technological change on manufacturing and workforce development, such as David Autor and Elisabeth Reynolds (2020), are warning that the Covid-19 pandemic is "poised to reshape labor markets along at least four axes: telepresence, urban de-densification, employment concentration in large firms, and general automation forcing" and that this recalibration could result in greater inequality in countries like the United States. Their assessment of the post-Covid labor environment is worth citing at length:

> Although these changes will have long-run efficiency benefits, they will exacerbate economic pain in the short and medium terms for the least economically secure workers in our economy, particular those in the rapidly growing but never-highly-paid personal services sector . . . Despite our concerns about the distributional consequences of advancing technologies, until the Covid crisis began, we were sanguine about the prospects for ongoing employment growth, even in the face of lackluster wage growth . . . [But] if anything, the crisis has simply brought the possibility of an increasingly automation-intensive future closer to

the present . . . The Covid crisis has shaken our core confidence that the U.S. labor market, caught between the demographic pincers of a swelling retiree population and a flagging fertility rate, would almost inevitably experience structurally tight labor markets for many years to come. No one foresaw that a global pandemic would spur an overnight revolution in telepresence that may upend commuting patterns and business travel, and hence dent demand in rapidly growing—though never highly paid—personal service occupations. Tight labor markets no longer appear inevitable—and certainly their return is some years off—which raises greater concerns about the trajectory of the polarized U.S. labor market. (2, 5)

One might reasonably assume that these trends would be limited to wealthy, even predominantly "Global North," countries with substantial social programs in place to "soften" any turmoil created by technological progress or disruption to entire industry sectors. However, "Global South" countries and other developing regions that rely on industrial production for job growth and economic vitality are also likely to experience rapid change. Technological advances in the field of robotics could make tasks that involve mobility and dexterity less human-centered (Wike & Stokes, 2018). Meatpacking plants, for example, are already expanding their use of robots and other forms of mechanization after precarious working conditions and vulnerabilities to the food supply chain were exposed by the Covid-19 pandemic (Motlteni, 2020). Hence, any occupation that involves logistics, construction, service, or office and administrative support could be at "high risk," as defined by Frey and Osborne (2017), for disruption. While it is true that industries reliant on cheap labor may be disinclined to invest in costly equipment, a confluence of social pressure and new economic policies might expedite an embrace of robotics comparable to the 1980s transformation of the automobile industry (Hunt, 1990).

Having discussed "high-risk" occupations at length, it is valuable to recognize which occupations Frey and Osborne identified as "low-risk" occupations. One class of "low-risk" labor is any job that requires a deep understanding of the dynamics of human interaction, especially when it comes to social and intercultural communication (Gut, Wilczewski, & Gorbaniuk, 2017; Ladegaard & Jenks, 2015). These positions are likely to be found in business, education, medicine, and various forms of media enterprises.

Another class of "low-risk" employment concerns the development of new ideas and/or the implementation of new innovations, such as found in science, engineering, and fine arts disciplines. To be competitive in one of these two broad employment classes, individuals must develop four proficiencies: (1) expert knowledge in a given field; (2) the ability to pursue research and development; (3) the ability to engage in interactive problem solving; and (4) the capacity to adapt to changes in communication technologies.

Other projections are less ominous about the future of employment but nonetheless indicate that significant change is on the horizon. Researchers at the McKinsey Institute, for example, studied the work activities of over 800 occupations in the U.S. economy (Manyika et al., 2017a). After compiling a list that itemized the time spent on more than 2,000 work activities, they determined the feasibility of technological automation. The McKinsey authors assert that less than 5% of all occupations in the United States could be fully automated through the adaptation or evolution of current technology. However, they caution that automation, specifically, and technological innovation, more broadly, is likely to impact virtually every occupation, from gardeners to CEOs. The relative extent to which automation and innovation affects the daily work lives of individuals is the real question. In this regard, education is viewed as the "least susceptible to automation" as the "essence of teaching is deep expertise and experience, and complex interactions with other people. Together, those two categories [are] the least automatable [and] account for about half of the activities in the education sector" (46).

> Automation could exacerbate a skills gap, even as it touches all occupations. There is already a growing divide in income advancement and employment opportunities between high-skill workers and those who are low- and medium-skill. In the past two decades, there has been a clear pattern of consistent job growth for high-skill workers and little or no growth for low- and middle-skill ones. For example, in 1981, college-educated workers in the United States earned a 48 percent wage premium over high school graduates. By 2005, that premium had risen to 97 percent—in other words, an American college graduate earns almost twice as much as a high school graduate. The growing gap between productivity and wages is not new, but automation could accelerate the process. (112–113)

In a follow-up report, Manyika and colleagues (2017b) emphasize that the effects of automation will be disparate, but they focus on the ages of workers rather than the socioeconomic dimensions:

> The changes in net occupational growth or decline imply that a very large number of people may need to shift occupational categories and learn new skills in the years ahead. The shift could be on a scale not seen since the transition of the labor force out of agriculture in the early 1900s in the United States and Europe, and more recently in China. But unlike those earlier transitions, in which young people left farms and moved to cities for industrial jobs, the challenge, especially in advanced economies, will be to retrain midcareer workers. There are few precedents in which societies have successfully retrained such large numbers of people. Frictions in the labor markets—including cultural norms regarding gender stereotypes in work and geographic mismatches between workers and jobs—could also impede the transition. (9)

Assuming these projected developments and conclusions are accurate, it should be apparent that higher education will need to play a key role in developing the creative, emotional, and social intelligence skills of college students from all backgrounds, work experiences, and ages.[7] Workers of all ages will also need to learn how to interact with digital media, machines, and technological advancements in a more comprehensive and time-effective fashion. If higher education does not rethink how education is delivered and how curricula are formulated in variety of disciplines and academic fields, a significant percentage of youth and working-age adults may not have viable skills for the labor markets of today and the future.

3. Massification versus Elitism in Higher Education

As innovation increasingly becomes intertwined with workforce development, many national higher education systems are likely to engage in deliberate massification strategies that reflect their changing labor demands (Altbach, Reisberg, & de Wit, 2017; Alves & Tomlinson, 2021; Wu & Hawkins, 2018). Many influential administrators and academics, such as Michael Crow and William Dabars (2020), have argued that "despite diminished public support, research-grade colleges and universities must begin in earnest to expand enrollment capacity" (2) in order to expand opportunity and promote socioeconomic mobility in wealthy countries like the United States. Nevertheless, higher education systems in developing countries may be under the greatest pressure to develop massification strategies. Without innovative ideas, these nations may find it impossible to build capacity while simultaneously funding research and other important institutional activities. For example, Brunner (2013) has observed that Latin American countries will likely experience an influx of students "from households with reduced economic, social, and cultural capital" (5), creating problems for higher education systems already lacking in resources. "Innovative concepts" will also be necessary "to respond to social demands and ambitions, which aspire to leave poverty, authoritarianism, violence, and inequalities behind" (7). East Asia is another region that will require innovative thinking to confront incipient challenges. As noted by Postiglione (2011), the governance and administrative systems of universities in China, Mongolia, and Vietnam have heavy bureaucracies that can result in a waste of vital resources. They may be unable to help indigent students complete a tertiary-level education without innovative reforms in the coming years that prioritize access, student adjustment, and new teaching methods.

At the same time, prominent universities throughout the world are interested in cultivating a "global" brand so they can expand their reach beyond the traditional nation-state borders within which institutions typically functioned. Elsewhere we have written about different waves of globalization that have taken place in higher education since the 1990s (Tierney & Lanford, 2015). The "first wave" of globalization was distinguished by student mobility. American students have a long history of studying in a different country for a single semester through "study abroad" programs. The number of U.S. students who have taken advantage of such programs, though, has grown tremendously, with 71,000 enrolling in a study abroad semester during the 1991–1992 academic year and 283,332 studying abroad in 2011–2012 (Institute of International Education, 2013). During the same time period, the total number of international students studying for a postsecondary credential rose from 1.3 million to nearly 4.3 million (OECD, 2013). Geopolitical conflicts, ongoing international disparities in Covid-19 infection rates and vaccine rollouts, and sustainability concerns about the impact of international travel on the environment make it difficult to envision how many students will be traveling to international destinations over the next few years. Nevertheless, by 2025, it is estimated that as many as 7.6 million students will be taking classes at a college or university in a different country (Kim, 2010). At the very least, a period of dynamic change concerning enrollment patterns is likely on the horizon.

The "second wave" of globalization has seen a decided uptick in the number of researchers, programs, and institutions that either study, work, or form a collaborative partnership with an institutional entity in a different country. One useful example concerns the number of international branch campuses developed in recent years. International branch campuses are commonly defined as institutions that have a physical campus owned and operated by a foreign institution, generally in the name of the foreign institution, and offer both administrative and teaching staff, as well as in-person coursework that leads to an accredited postsecondary credential (Lanford & Tierney, 2016). One of the earliest tabulations of international branch campuses was conducted in 2002 by the Observatory on Borderless Higher Education (OBHE); they determined that 18 international branch campuses were operational at that time (Garrett, 2002). A follow-up study by OBHE determined that, in the space of 4 years, 82 international branch campuses were in existence during the year 2006 (Verbik & Merkley, 2006). As of November 2021, a survey conducted by the Cross-Border Education Research Team at the State University of New York at Albany determined that 306 international branch campuses were active in 37 countries.

The motivations behind establishing such a complex and risky venture mirror the motivations behind international partnerships. From the perspective of the host country, international branch campuses can facilitate greater research collaboration across borders, enhance a country's prestige through an affiliation with a globally recognized institution, expand the capacity of the higher education sector, and/or develop a national workforce that is relevant to a knowledge-intensive economy (Becker, 2009; Knight, 2011). Meanwhile, exporting institutions have been similarly motivated by self-interest, enticed by the promise of economic gain, the potential for stronger international connections, the recruitment of highly desired foreign students, the potential to expand alumni reach, and/or a desire to gain influence in an emerging higher education marketplace (Becker, 2009; Edelstein & Douglass, 2012; Lanford, 2020; Sidhu, 2009; Wilkins & Huisman, 2012).

Unfortunately, though, the motivations behind these global partnerships and international ventures rarely appear to embrace two concepts also essential to the mission of many colleges and universities: social justice and increased student access. We have already demonstrated that both Global South and Global North countries need more people to complete higher education—and with more comprehensive learning experiences than a vocational program might typically provide. However, access remains a key barrier for many low-income students around the world. In the United States, for instance, the average student-to-counselor ratio in the public high school system is 464 to 1.[8] In some states with large numbers of low-income students, such as California, the ratio is as high as 609 to 1, even after substantial investments that added 2,220 new counselors over 8 years.[9] This extreme disparity affects the ability of students to access essential information and support for the college application process. It also presents a major hurdle in facilitating college admission for millions of marginalized students who are frequently the first in their families to consider attending college.

Perhaps most distressingly, nearly two-thirds of the selective colleges and universities in the United States that have the greatest potential to facilitate economic opportunities have reduced the proportion of enrolled low-income students since the 1990s. Disparities are most prevalent at Ivy League institutions, where a student from a family in the top 1% of the nation's income scale is 77 times more likely to attend an Ivy League university than a student from the bottom quintile. At the nation's most prestigious public universities, students from families in the bottom 20% of the income scale constitute only 6% of the total enrollment (Burd, 2017).

Given these trends, it is little wonder that higher education institutions are looking to alleviate financial pressures relating to student support and teacher pedagogy through the adoption and implementation of potentially innovative digital tools. To be sure, digital tools can be thoughtfully deployed in a way that increases the efficiency of educational environments. For example, online learning has the potential to decrease the costs of higher education, especially for students where college options are limited by geography and/or insufficient transportation (Deming et al., 2015). Furthermore, the ways in which large datasets and predictive analytics can be employed to support educational outcomes are just starting to be explored and better understood (Daniel, 2015; Dede, Ho, & Mitros, 2016). We will discuss the potential for these and other possibly innovative ideas to take root in secondary and postsecondary education later in the book. Here we will argue, however, that a deep understanding of diffusion theory is essential for the successful implementation of any innovative idea or instrument.

To be sure, not every higher education system will face the demands of massification, as some have already jumped ahead of the curve. From 1986 to 2012, the total university student population of Taiwan increased from 345,736 to 1,259,490 total students due to a deliberate admissions strategy that prioritized access over the perception of exclusivity. The university acceptance rate in Taiwan was approximately 20% in the 1970s; today, it is closer to 90%, which is one of the highest proportions in all of Asia. Concurrently, Taiwan has also massively increased its Masters and Doctoral programs such that one of every 3.7 undergraduates eventually registers in a graduate school program. In one 10-year period (1996 to 2006), the percentage of doctoral students enrolled in various disciplines jumped by 244 percent (Chou, 2014; Yang, 2012).

Some have argued that Taiwan's process of massification has been too accessible—and that it illustrates a lack of competitiveness within the sector (Hsueh, 2018). As a result, Taiwan started to shift its focus to establishing an "elite" sector of institutions in 2003, with the launch of the World Class Research University Project. Similar to the Ivy League in the United States or the C9 in China, Taiwan hopes to have 12 universities achieve international reputations for excellence through the allocation of additional funding for research. Other countries, such as Qatar, have invested in "Education Cities" that host international branch campuses from institutions representing a variety of foreign countries. Through such an education hub, the hope is that entrepreneurial activities will strengthen the bonds between elite institutions and their hosts while transferring much-desired intellectual capital that can be used for the development of other institutions years down the road. For these nations, the quality of higher education, rather than the quantity, may be the primary point of emphasis in the near term.

International and national ranking systems, along with other comparative indicators, have invigorated competition between individual universities and national higher education sectors. A number of stakeholders, including administrators, faculty, and students, now make important decisions about higher education based on tables and rankings produced by governments and independent media outlets (Hazelkorn, 2008). Seemingly, every institution now aspires to world-class status, as observed by Salmi (2009):

> No longer are countries comfortable with developing their tertiary education systems to serve their local or national communities . . . These world-class universities are now more than just cultural and educational institutions—they are points of pride and comparison among nations that view their own status in relation to other nations. World-class standards may be a reasonable goal for some institutions in many countries, but they are likely not relevant, cost-effective, or efficient for many others (x–xi).

Other outcomes related to massification and workforce development, however, are not quite as easy to quantify and do not match the aspirations of many research universities. For instance, a national higher education system interested in fostering greater democratic participation might prioritize community service to encourage informed civic engagement by younger generations. Likewise, student development that results in improved regional economic vitality might be especially desirable for a nation transitioning from an industrial economy to a knowledge economy. To date, however, none of the major ranking systems even attempt to evaluate such activities. An institution hoping to encourage such activities would have to make a concerted, principled stand to develop its own internal metrics and resist external pressures, even at the peril of losing prestige.

Thus, the pressures of massification will be circumscribed by the resources mandated by world-class aspirations. Across the globe, it remains to be seen how many countries will continue to allocate their resources to improve their standing in the superficial metrics assessed by rankings and tables. How quality is defined, however, is still likely to be related to the competitive pressures presented by a knowledge economy that prizes innovation.

Concluding Thoughts

Higher education has confronted problems related to economic transformation, workforce development, and massification in previous decades, but the urgency with which higher education is expected to respond to these changes by both government and the private sector is rather extraordinary. As we will discuss in subsequent chapters, the charter of the government, society, and universities has been weakened over the past few decades by decreased public subsidies for higher education and a widespread embrace of neoliberal philosophies. Universities have been encouraged to seek out private and international funding opportunities by courting industry research collaborations and cross-border partnerships. Moreover, activities once peripheral to the mission of universities, such as athletics, have assumed core status due to their potential for commercialization and financial profit.

Innovative solutions will be necessary for universities to maintain their compact with government, align their programs with public objectives, and find solutions to societal problems. However, as we noted in Chapter 1, it will become apparent over the course of this book that we are not "innovation boosters," as if everything new is to be embraced and everything old is to be viewed as outdated. As argued in our discussion of the 2007–2008 financial crisis, the relentless association of "innovation" with "positive development" has caused many within higher education to dismiss the concept as a hollow marketing term with little useful meaning. We will suggest, however, that a nuanced understanding of innovation as a concept, as well as critical engagement with the implications of innovation, is necessary if individuals and institutions are to evolve in a valuable and productive manner.

In Chapter 3, we catalyze a conversation about innovation through a selective overview of how innovation has been viewed by two prominent theorists. Joseph Schumpeter's early 20th-century warnings of "creative destruction" will be compared with Clayton Christensen's contemporary rhetoric of "disruptive innovation," and their relative merits for higher education and greater society will be discussed. In Chapter 4, we will argue that an analysis of higher education's problems through the lens of neoliberalism and New Public Management is incomplete and counterproductive to organizational innovation. Instead, we will suggest that innovation needs a broader conceptual approach that embraces multiple missions, venerable traditions, and diverse perspectives that have stimulated creativity and innovative production.

Over the next three chapters, we will build to this conceptual understanding of mindful innovation. Afterward, in Chapter 5, we will provide working definitions for innovation, creativity, and entrepreneurship in higher education. Chapter 6 will draw upon empirical research to develop a framework for stimulating mindful innovation. Chapter 7 will similarly present a framework for planning, developing, and implementing a culture of mindful innovation in colleges and universities. Then, in Chapters 8 and 9, we will contend that U.S. higher education, for much of the 20th century, was more innovative than commonly perceived. Through the tenets of academic freedom, tenure, shared governance, and institutional autonomy, colleges and universities fostered the conditions for creative and innovative inquiry that propelled the rise of American higher education in the 20th century.

Chapter 3

From Creative Destruction to Disruption

Evolving Perceptions of Innovation

"Can capitalism survive? No, I do not think it can."

The Origins of Creative Destruction

It may come as a surprise to some that these words come from the pen of Joseph A. Schumpeter, an Austrian political economist widely regarded as the "prophet of innovation" for his memorable depiction of "creative destruction." Those familiar with his life history would recognize how a turbulent career forged by the geopolitical events of the early 20th century might shape such an opinion. In 1888, Schumpeter was born in the Moravia region of today's Czech Republic to German-speaking parents. At the age of 4, Joseph's father passed away, and his mother moved him to Vienna, then the center of the Austro-Hungarian Empire. This move shaped much of Schumpeter's life trajectory, as he was able to gain admission to the most prestigious prep school in Vienna (with significant help from a 65-year-old stepfather who was a retired Austrian army general). Later, he earned a PhD in law from the University of Vienna, studying with Eugen Böhm Ritter von Bawerk, a renowned capital theorist who served as the Austrian Minister of Finance for various terms between 1895 and 1904. Schumpeter's interests spanned several emerging disciplines at the time, as he studied economics, history, and sociology, along with his civil and Roman law coursework.

Not only did Schumpeter benefit from the rich intellectual and economic environment of Vienna—his residence was six blocks from the University of Vienna and roughly 100 feet from the Imperial Parliament—but he also developed a cosmopolitan perspective. Ultimately, he moved 23 times, between 11 cities and 7 countries, before writing his most famous work, *Capitalism, Socialism, and Democracy*, in 1942. During that period, he held faculty positions at four universities: the University of Czernowitz (1909–1911), the University of Graz (1912–1914), the University of Bonn (1925–1932), and Harvard University (1932–1950). He also served as a visiting professor at Columbia University from 1913 to 1914 (during which he received an honorary degree at the age of 26) and the Tokyo College of Commerce in 1931.

Schumpeter's wide-ranging interests impelled him to accept several positions outside of academia, as well, and these experiences informed his view of history and economics. After witnessing the horrors of World War I, he took up the thankless job of serving as German-Austria's Minister of Finance in 1919, hoping to stem hyperinflation through free trade, foreign loans, and programs designed to encourage entrepreneurship. The reforms were nonetheless hampered by terms from the Treaty of Versailles limiting governmental action by the Austrian state. Thus, when Schumpeter was ousted from the cabinet after 7 months, he took on a new challenge: incorporating the newly formed Beidermann Bank and serving as its inaugural president from 1921 to 1924. This fleeting period of exceptional personal wealth, however, was cut short by the Vienna Stock Market crash of 1924, which caused Schumpeter to lose virtually all of his savings and incur substantial debt.

Schumpeter's next move—a chair faculty position in economics at the University of Bonn—seemed to portend a period of stability in his life, only to be cut short by personal tragedy. A mere 8 months after relocating to Bonn, Schumpeter's mother passed away, and six weeks afterward, his second wife died in childbirth. Bankrupt and without the two most beloved figures in his life, Schumpeter wrote to a friend, "Everything looks so grim now that I do not care what happens . . . I may have deserved much, but this, no" (McCraw, 2008).

In short, Schumpeter experienced two world wars, personal tragedies, and a variety of stock market crashes and radical inflationary periods in Europe and United States that not only belied his academic successes but also informed his academic work. There is a tendency to view current events through the prisms of globalization, rapid technological change, and a global pandemic and assume that no previous time in history has experienced such rapid upheaval. Schumpeter, however, was no stranger to accelerated political and economic change, and his critique of capitalism was not the work of a clandestine communist in free market regalia. Rather, Schumpeter was attempting to make sense of the seemingly continuous cycles of progress and devastation that he personally witnessed in his different professions and documented through his scholarly research. By 1932, Schumpeter, in an article entitled "Development," had identified "novelty" as the defining feature of innovation, arguing that both time and hindsight were necessary to gauge the distinction between a novel product and a truly innovative one (Carlile & Lakhani, 2011). Ten years later, Schumpeter (1942/2003) merged his vision of novelty and innovation with a trenchant critique of the capitalist system that has ramifications for understanding the contemporary rhetoric of "disruption":

> The essential point to grasp is that in dealing with capitalism we are dealing with an evolutionary process . . . Capitalism, then, is by nature a form or method of economic change and not only never is, but never can be, stationary. And this evolutionary character of the capitalist process is not merely due to the fact that economic life goes on in a social and natural environment . . . this fact is important and these changes (wars, revolutions, and so on) often condition industrial change, but they are not its prime movers. . . . The fundamental impulse that sets and keeps the capitalist engine in motion comes from the new consumers' goods, the new methods of production or transportation, the new markets, the new forms of industrial organization that capitalist enterprise creates. (82–83)

In essence, Schumpeter was neither a proponent nor a detractor of innovation. He was a sober critic who encouraged readers to grasp the cultural, social, political, and economic implications of the "evolutionary character of the capitalist process." Thus, when Schumpeter answers his own question—"Can capitalism survive? No, I do not think it can"—he is cautioning the reader that innovation could initiate a "process of creative destruction" (83). Therein lies an essential paradox. Institutions need innovation for their competitive advantage and survival. However, those same innovations are capable of inducing economic and societal revolutions, from which successful innovators could assert monopolistic positions, market dominance, and excessive profit.

As stated by Schumpeter (1942/2008), "the actual and prospective performance of the capitalist system is such as to negate the idea of its breaking down under the weight of economic failure, but that its very success undermines the social institutions which protect it" (61). This focus on social institutions has been somewhat lost in discussions around innovation. Nevertheless, in recent years, we have witnessed the effects that economic disruption, through innovation, can have on social cohesion, as well as wealth and income inequality.

Higher Education is in "Deep Crisis"—Do Something!

Fast forwarding to 1997, Peter Drucker, a business guru who had an extraordinary impact on the philosophies and operational values underlying 20th-century corporate management, famously predicted that "higher education [was] in deep crisis":

> Thirty years from now the big university campuses will be relics. Universities won't survive. It's as large a change as when we first got the printed book. Do you realize that the cost of higher education has risen as fast as the cost of health care? And for the middle-class family, college education for their children is as much of a necessity as is medical care—without it, the kids have no future. Such totally uncontrollable expenditures, without any visible improvement in either the content or the quality of education, means that the system is rapidly becoming untenable. (Lenzner & Johnson, 1997)

Almost 25 years later, how does Drucker's prediction look? International higher education scholars, such as Simon Marginson (2016), have observed that "worldwide participation in higher education . . . is growing at an unprecedented rate" (1). The UNESCO Gross Tertiary Enrollment Rate increases by 1% each year. Countries where more than one half of recent high school graduates immediately enter higher education used to be restricted to a handful of high-income economies located primarily in North America and Europe. Today, however, almost every emerging high-income country, especially in South America and the Caribbean, as well as several middle-income countries (with a per capita gross national income between $1,005 and $12,235, such as Albania, Turkey, and Ukraine), are witnessing at least 50% of their secondary school cohorts entering colleges and universities immediately after graduation (UNESCO, 2015). In some countries, the growth has been staggering; South Korea, for example, has witnessed an increase in higher education participation from 7.2% in 1971 to 98.4% in 2013 (Marginson, 2016; UNESCO, 2015). As we discussed in the preceding chapter, higher education systems throughout the world are seeking to expand access to colleges and universities in response to the labor demands of the 21st century.

Some might reasonably counter that Drucker's predictions were limited to higher education in the United States. However, even after a substantial consolidation period for public colleges and universities, as well as a wave of mass closings in the for-profit colleges and universities (FPCUs) sector since 2010, the United States had, as of the 2018–2019 academic year, only six fewer 2- and 4-year campuses today than in 1998–1999 (NCES, 2019a). The United States had around 14.51 million students enrolled in public and private colleges in 1998, and approximately 19.66 million students enrolled in 2018 (NCES, 2019b). According to the Academic Ranking of World Universities (published in Shanghai, China) and the Quacquarelli Symonds World University Rankings and Times Higher Education World University Rankings (published in the United Kingdom), the United States still has roughly half of the world's top hundred universities. It is true that more than 1,230 campuses closed from 2014 to 2018, but nearly 88% of those closures were for-profit institutions (Vasquez & Bauman, 2019). A handful of poorly endowed liberal arts colleges, especially those with enrollments with less than 1,000 students, are likely to face severe financial challenges in the future (Grawe, 2018; Parthenon Group, 2016). However, higher education institutions throughout the United States have proven to be remarkably resilient.

One could argue that this resilience has never been better demonstrated than during the Covid-19 pandemic. When Covid-19 first began to spread throughout the world in February 2020, the disease appeared to instigate a perfect storm of existential problems for higher education. Not only did student enrollment decline and tuition revenue diminish but students were not able to live in residential halls, buy meal plans, or pay auxiliary fees— each of which have become key sources of revenue for many institutions. Fearing a decline in tax revenues, American states cut $74 billion from their higher education budgets in 2020 and have largely failed to restore funding in 2021 (Friga, 2021). The state of Colorado cut funding for higher education by 58%, a stunning decision softened only by federal emergency funds. In total, Paul Friga has estimated that U.S. institutions lost $183 billion during the first year of the pandemic. Moreover, colleges and universities were unable to monetize campus facilities by hosting conferences, summer music and athletics camps, and other activities. And despite ominous warnings from normally measured experts that as many as 1,000 colleges would fail to survive the pandemic, only 10 institutions—all small, private colleges that had prior financial difficulties—closed or consolidated with other institutions between March 2020 and January 2021 (Natow, 2021). It is admittedly possible that additional closures will occur if the pandemic drags on for a couple of years longer as a result of widespread virus variants or other unforeseen developments. Nevertheless, we struggle to see an "end of the higher education world" scenario coming true, particularly given the demonstrated ability of higher education institutions to survive during the austere environment generated by the pandemic.

Signs of a Fractured System?

1. Student Debt

Even amidst the explosion of matriculation in higher education institutions worldwide, we appreciate Peter Drucker's concerns, especially those pertaining to funding, expenditures, quality, consumer confidence, and the "over-education" of graduates in certain saturated fields of study. Since 2008, state funding for public colleges and universities in the United States has fallen by approximately $9 billion. As a result, the annual tuition students pay to attend a 4-year public university has risen by an average of 35%, and tuition has risen by more than 60% in eight states (Mitchell, Leachman, & Masterson, 2017).[1] Correlation does not equal causation, but other studies have indicated that students generally pay an additional $318 in tuition expenses whenever $1,000 is cut from public funding for higher education (Webber, 2017). Hence, it is unavoidable to surmise that, as public support for higher education has precipitously dropped throughout the United States, the burden of paying for college has been forced onto the college-goer. This statement is backed by evidence from student loan data. Adjusting for inflation, U.S. students at colleges and universities held

$7.6 billion of debt to fund their studies in 1970–1971. By the 2012–2013 academic year, U.S. students and graduates held $930 billion in student loan debt (Baum, 2015; Fry, 2014). As of September 2020, total student loan debt totaled $1.57 trillion (Looney, 2021).[2] Reduced public spending on higher education even appears to have a negative impact on degree completion, particularly at institutions (like community colleges) where large numbers of students are either adult learners or need to balance full-time employment with college coursework (Zhao, 2018). Therefore, not only has college become vastly more expensive, but the quality of education, as evaluated by student retention and completion statistics, has arguably deteriorated.

California's vaunted Master Plan for Higher Education in 1960 once claimed that there was a place in a public college for any citizen who wanted a degree. Obviously, there were discriminatory flaws in the plan. Students from lower-class backgrounds, many of whom were disproportionately from minoritized communities, ended up going to open-access colleges. Meanwhile, the children of the wealthy, who were overwhelmingly white, entered the University of California (UC) system. In both cases, though, "tuition" was rarely mentioned. Students might have needed to pay "fees" for extracurricular materials or activities, but the state made every attempt to cover the cost of college under a belief that access to higher education was a public good worth funding (Callan, 2012; Marginson, 2016a).[3] As of 2014–2015, the average college student who attended a UC institution would accumulate $21,018 in debt.[4] As far back as 2009, California families in the lowest income quintile had to spend 52.5% of their income to attend a California public 2-year institution (Finney et al., 2014). One can imagine that families today would have to incur much greater debt to graduate with a 2-year degree, much less a 4-year degree from an institution in the UC system.

How can one not be concerned with the future of higher education when costs have risen astronomically, and many students now fall deeply in debt? In 1989, the average cost of a 4-year degree was $52,892, when adjusted for inflation, yet the average cost of a 4-year degree during the 2015–2016 academic year was $104,480 (Maldonado, 2018). In fact, tuition has risen almost eight times faster than average annual growth in wages.[5] As of the fourth quarter of 2018, the totality of student debt in the United States was $1.569 trillion,[6] and many worry that the next financial crash could come about because of consumers' inability to repay their loans (e.g., Phillips & Russell, 2018).

2. The Public Perception of Higher Education

According to recent Gallup Polls, the public perception of higher education has also become more negative over the past couple of years. In 2015, 57% of American adults had "a great deal" or "quite a lot" of confidence in colleges and universities. However, in 2018, only 48% felt this way (Jaschik, 2018). As recently as 1968, John Dewey, an influential educational philosopher, was admired enough to be recognized by the U.S. Postal Service with a 30-cent postage stamp, and his ideas were admired in other countries (Bruno-Jofré & Schriewer, 2012; Rogacheva, 2016; Turan, 2000). Woodrow Wilson, a former president of Princeton, went on to become President of the United States in 1913. Father Theodore Hesburgh, President of the University of Notre Dame from 1952 to 1987, gained national renown as Chair of the U.S. Civil Rights Commission and was one of America's most admired citizens. Although some academics still reach beyond the academy—Professors Paul Wellstone in Minnesota and Ben Sasse in Nebraska were elected to the U.S. Senate—the most noted person in higher education in 2020 was a football coach: Nick Saban at the University of Alabama. Whereas a college degree was once seen as a guarantee for a good job, and a step up for those who were poor, a great deal of disagreement surrounds the worth of academe today. Some will argue that there are too many participants in higher education, and over-credentialing has in effect brought us to the point where those with a college degree are pizza delivery drivers (Vedder, 2012). Others, such as Peter Thiel, even pay students to avoid college, instead encouraging them to immediately focus on a "radical innovation that [might] benefit society" (Clynes, 2016). Regrettably, although many of Peter Thiel's protégés managed to raise impressive amounts of venture capital for topical energy sprays and budget hotels, none of them managed to create the "radical innovation" that could have a far-reaching, positive impact on society. As a result, an entrepreneur who is a distinguished fellow at Carnegie Mellon's School of Engineering in Silicon Valley led one article with the headline: "Peter Thiel promised flying cars; we got caffeine spray instead" (Wadhwa, 2013).

Traditional higher education also was the only game in town for the last half century. The question for those in the middle and upper classes when they graduated from high school was not *should* they go to college, but *where* to go. But then, in the 1970s, competitors appeared. FPCUs at first seemed like earnest competitors until their disreputable marketing practices; flagrant disregard for state and federal regulations; atrocious outcomes relating to student retention, low rates of employment, and meager earnings; and reliance on federal money to fund the massive loan debts of their own students were chronicled by numerous researchers (Angulo, 2016; Armona, Chakrabarti, & Lovenheim, 2018; Cellini & Koedel, 2017; Cellini & Turner, 2018; Cottom, 2017; Kelchen, 2017; Shireman, 2017; Shireman & Cochrane, 2017). Campuses began closing and declaring bankruptcy. From a high of 1,424 institutions in 2013–2014, only 742 FPCUs remained in 2018–2019, and many more are expected to close over the next few years (NCES, 2019a). Other once-promising competitors, such as the multistate-sponsored Western Governor's University, have not yielded institutional progeny.

The part of Drucker's crystal ball, then, pertaining to the "untenable" costs of higher education has been proven right. Even while revenue dropped due to state finances, the costs of higher education rose, and a college degree is no longer a surefire path to gainful employment. At the same time, we still need to acknowledge that college degree holders have much lower unemployment rates than non–college graduates, and their wages are much higher (Johnson, Meija, & Bohn, 2015). In fact, college graduates earn approximately one million dollars more than high school graduates over their working lifetimes (Abel & Deitz, 2014). The benefits of a college degree are more than purely financial, as well. Over their lives, college graduates will more likely participate in elections, volunteer for charity work, contribute to the civic spheres of their communities, and help their children enroll in college (Trostel & Chase, 2015).

3. DEMOGRAPHIC AND INSTITUTIONAL INSTABILITIES

Perhaps even more concerning, this tandem of spiraling costs and a decrease in consumer confidence are demographic and institutional instabilities that could result in plummeting enrollments and systemic failures within certain sectors within higher education. Moody's has pointed out that about a quarter of private colleges are running deficits (Lederman, 2018a). These are institutions largely dependent upon tuition derived from a stable or increasing enrollment. The opposite is happening. Even when campuses have tried to be creative, they have wrongly assumed that "cheaply delivered" credentials, such as online master's and professional degree programs, would be their magic elixir (Marcus, 2017a). Unfortunately, such programs' effect on institutional finances has been limited. Other Western colleges and universities have controversially viewed international students as "cash cows," under the expectation that wealthy foreign parents (or sometimes the students' home governments) will pay full—or even enhanced—tuition costs (Cantwell, 2015; Choudaha, 2017; Robertson, 2011). However, the xenophobia represented by the Trump administration's policies on international students, particularly during the Covid-19 pandemic, has given many governments and parents second thoughts about sending their children abroad (Leiber, 2019; Venegas et al., 2017). Moreover, international students increasingly no longer feel the need to travel to foreign countries when Western-educated faculty are already teaching in their home institutions and on international branch campuses (Kretovics, 2018; Lanford, 2020). The result is a multiyear decline in foreign student enrollment—from a high of 119,262 undergraduate and 126,516 graduate students in 2016 to 108,539 undergraduate and 117,960 graduate students in 2018—precisely at a time when many institutions need more international students to stay afloat and contribute to research (Hackman & Belkin, 2018). The decline from 2016 to 2017 was 3.3%, and the decline from 2017 to 2018 was 6.6%. Sharper declines will have a damaging impact on the intellectual, cultural, and financial lives of U.S. campuses.

Demographics also are not in higher education's favor. Traditional students (between the ages of 18 and 24) are starting to decline, and within a decade we will see significant declines, particularly in the northeastern and midwestern United States (Grawe, 2018; Marcus, 2017b). At the same time, the proportion of students who are first-generation and low-income is likely to increase. When we also take into account that the real price of tuition is not actually the real price—the average tuition discount rate is almost 50% for first-time full-time freshmen (NACBU, 2018)—it is apparent that there is cause for real concern. Rural campuses, where population is likely to drop, and small campuses with enrollments less than 1,000 are particularly at risk.

One can also be gloomy about student involvement. Although we correctly stated that more students participate today in higher education than a generation ago, a deeper dive into the enrollment also has cause for concern in different postsecondary sectors. The days of students devoting their full attention to their studies is largely over. A study published in 2015 by Georgetown University's Center on Education and the Workforce revealed that approximately 40% of undergraduate students and 76% of graduate students work at least 30 hours a week. Even while working long hours, 45% of students aged 16 to 29 earned 200% or less of the poverty threshold ($23,540), making loan debt a virtual certainty for such students (Carnevale et al., 2015). Just before the pandemic, around one-third of all college students were participating in online learning through at least one class (Lederman, 2018b), whereas when Drucker made his prediction, the internet was in its infancy.

We also know that closures and consolidations of higher education institutions, while not common, are likely to increase. To be sure, the numbers remain tiny in the grand scheme of things—before the pandemic, Moody's demonstrated that private colleges were closing at a rate of approximately 11 per year (Seltzer, 2018)—but they should still be cause for concern. One might reasonably ask if these signs of a fractured system—student debt, the negative public perception of higher education, and demographic and institutional instabilities—could foreshadow imminent disruption for higher education.

One Diagnosis: Disruptive Innovation

Writers who herald disruption seem to follow in Drucker's footsteps, rather than heed the arguably more nuanced counsel of Joseph Schumpeter. For about a decade, Clayton Christensen, the prominent Harvard business professor who developed the theory of disruptive innovation, has similarly predicted the mass collapse of higher education. In 2017, a reporter asked Christensen during a question-and-answer period at a Higher Education Summit sponsored by salesforce.org, "Do you still believe, as you've said before, that as many as half of all colleges and universities will be bankrupt or close within a decade?" Christensen answered with a stark "Yes" (Lederman, 2017). Indeed, Christensen in recent years has been even more precise; at the 2017 Innovation + Disruption Symposium in Higher Education, he argued, "If you're asking whether the providers get disrupted within a decade—I might bet that it takes nine years rather than 10" (Hess, 2018). One either is dazzled by such scientific precision or begins to think that those who claim "the end is near" are trying to create a hysteria similar to that created by previous prophets of doom. The prophecies prove false, but the prophets benefit.

Christensen's theory of disruptive innovation is similar to Schumpeter's view of "creative destruction" in that both focus on the relationship between innovation and the business sector, offering a cautionary tale to incumbent businesses dependent on legacy technologies. As stipulated by Christensen, a disruptive innovation begins its life by serving individuals in a given market who recognize and appreciate three specific qualities: (1) simplicity, (2) affordability, and (3) convenience. Perhaps even more importantly, the disruptive innovation offers a product or a service in a sector of the economy that previously excluded people due to prohibitive costs or high skill requirements. Usually, a disruptive innovation is of inferior quality when compared to incumbent products, especially in its first few incarnations. Hence, it requires continuous refinement and feedback from users. Nonetheless, disruptive innovations improve over time and start to be a viable option for larger numbers of people, especially if the costs remain affordable and the convenience is manifest through use. Over time, a mature implementation of the disruptive innovation can emerge as a dominant player in the market, and it ultimately creates an existential crisis for companies dependent on legacy technologies and/or sustainable innovations for survival.

Disruptive innovation theory has had a profound influence on business scholarship and contemporary discourse concerning the intersection of industry and technology. Many in higher education have worried that colleges and universities will become the next "legacy institution" supplanted by disruptive innovation, soon joining the ranks of CD players and department stores. Several commentators on higher education have written monographs and articles that predict the ascendance of disruptors, such as for-profit institutions and Massive Open Online Courses (MOOCs), that promise to offer a less expensive, simpler, and more expedient alternative to traditional colleges and universities (Christensen & Eyring, 2011; Christensen et al., 2011; Craig, 2015; Hixon, 2014; McCluskey & Winter, 2012). According to these writers, disruptors to the higher education *status quo* would provide "student-consumers" with pertinent and much-needed credentials for today's knowledge economy in a more efficient manner. These disruptors would also benefit governments looking to develop a better-skilled workforce while moving funds earmarked for higher education to other political and social imperatives.

While acknowledging that Christensen's theory offers useful insights into the factors that can shape adoption of an innovative product, we contend that higher education is different for four reasons.[7] First, higher education is a positional market (Hirsch, 1976) in which scarcity is induced by societal competition. If an individual possesses a highly valued positional good, their social status is elevated. What this means for higher education is that prestige often matters—especially since a diploma from a top-ranked university lasts for a lifetime. This statement is backed by substantial research concerning the overwhelming impact of institutional prestige on the hiring practices of prominent banks, consulting firms, and law firms (Rivera, 2011, 2015). Such institutional prestige, however, takes a long time for a college or university to develop, as it requires generations of alumni who achieve distinction in their fields and give back to their respective institutions, the cultivation of endowment funds through multiple decades, and impactful research that raises an institution's scholarly profile among its peers. This positional market explains why parents, as exemplified by the "Varsity Blues" admissions scandal, are willing to pay hundreds of thousands of dollars, and even risk prison sentences, to ensure that their children are admitted to prestigious universities—through dossiers of fake test scores, essays on experiences that never happened, and imaginary extracurricular activities (Jaschik, 2019; Medina, Benner, & Taylor, 2019). Although we decry rising tuition rates, many prestigious universities could potentially charge more and still have large incoming undergraduate classes of students from wealthy families, if higher education existed entirely in a free market.

Second, new research shows that legacy technologies, like the Swiss watch, can thrive as status goods even while potentially disruptive technologies, such as the digital watch, achieve mass production and distribution (King & Baatartogtokh, 2015; Raffaelli, 2015). If such a thesis is germane to higher education, then prestigious institutions with considerable accrued prestige will likely remain unaffected by disruptive technologies. However, open-access institutions that focus on marginalized communities might be impacted if the disruptors are able to find a cheaper, more convenient, and reasonably effective way to educate underserved students and offer them credentials recognized by employers.

Third, the relationship between higher education and government is vastly different from that of the technology sector frequently cited by Christensen for examples of disruptive innovations. An international perspective is helpful in considering this point. In most countries, the activities of colleges and universities are subject to the oversight of a Ministry of Postsecondary Education, or some similar governmental entity. Student enrollment in higher education is capped at a certain level and based on results of high-stakes examinations. Students who are successful in such exams are allowed to enroll in universities that are heavily subsidized by the government. As such, tuition costs at these state-subsidized institutions are much lower than the tuition costs at private institutions. While it is conceivable that an entrepreneur could develop a niche product to educate the substantial proportion of students who are purposefully kept out of these state-subsidized universities, a number of hurdles exist relating to accessibility, convenience, and affordability. Student technological literacy, as well as the high-tech infrastructure of a country, may be lacking. Finding a way to offer a privately supported degree that is less expensive than an established public incumbent that can rely on public coffers is challenging. The United States, on the other hand, is something of an anomaly in that a substantial proportion of its prestigious institutions are private. In the rest of the world, credentials from state-subsidized universities are invariably far more prestigious (and desired by employers) than those from private institutions.

Fourth, colleges and universities are fundamentally different from many businesses in that they serve multiple missions, such as workforce development, research into societal problems, the advancement of disciplinary knowledge, and community service. Disruptive innovation, when it is applied to higher education, typically focuses on just one mission—the teaching and learning aspects of colleges and universities. It is worth also mentioning that the majority of faculty in each of these institutions have shown a willingness to mindfully adopt and implement technology that caters to the needs of students, especially during the Covid-19 pandemic. We therefore assert that it is important for higher education professionals to interrogate any value system that romanticizes "disruption." The quest to create a simple, affordable, convenient, and accessible path to a degree is a laudable goal—and one we believe is essential for the continued health of higher education and society. Nevertheless, quality—as evaluated through the production of intellectually and artistically rigorous work—is also of central importance to the mission of any higher education institution. It is a simple matter to replace a 700-student class that meets in a lecture hall with an online class. Both environments provide a questionable educational experience, where quality is suspect. A well-run seminar, however, that sharpens students' critical thinking abilities through consistent feedback to weekly writing assignments is far more difficult to supplant. Bromidic academic and artistic production should be anathema to those who believe that a university's mission is to raise the level of discourse, educate students, and improve the human condition through innovation.

Some private venture capitalists and innovators may be frustrated at the measured pace many college and universities take to implement new ideas and technologies—especially if they have a vested financial interest in the adoption of an innovation. However, a restrained rollout is frequently the prudent decision, lest large numbers of students, staff, and instructors are adversely impacted by the premature adoption of a technology that stands to ruin an institution's carefully cultivated reputation and cause damage to the most vulnerable populations within an institution.

Christensen has gone on record as stating that his view of universities is deeply influenced by his personal observations of Harvard Business School, the institution with which he is most familiar. In particular, he has been a vocal critic of the roughly $75,000 per year that Harvard Business School charges for tuition, arguing that "our customers need so much money in opening salary to pay off their debt that we have overshot the salaries" companies are likely to pay graduates (Lederman, 2017). Christensen's criticism is fair, but it overlooks the fact that Harvard Business School is barely indicative of the higher education experiences that the majority of students have at regional universities and open-access community colleges in the United States, much less the experiences of students in other countries. As we have demonstrated, students throughout the country are already enrolled in degree programs at public institutions that are endeavoring to provide the most marketable credential at the lowest price.

The Rhetoric of Disruption: Gospel or Empty Jargon?

When we first began to write on disruptive innovation in 2016, we argued that the drive for disruption in higher education must be balanced by thorough considerations of an institution's stakeholders, its history, its identity, and its perceived strengths. Those points are important to reiterate here.[8] Christensen's theory of disruptive innovation is a useful prism through which administrators, researchers, and other stakeholders in higher education can potentially gain a deeper understanding of technological advances in today's rapidly changing, globalized environment. However, former students of Christensen have become increasingly dismayed that "[disruptive innovation] is frequently overused. Clearly, the term has sometimes become a cliché among those who don't understand. This is a reality of today's business environment" (Gilbert, 2014). Michelle Weise, a Senior Research Fellow at the Clayton Christensen Institute, has elaborated that "disruption" is one of the most overused buzzwords in education today:

> There is this tendency for pundits, policy makers and institutional leaders to take any kind of technological advancement, call it a "disruptive innovation," cram it into the classroom experience and then hope that somehow efficiencies are going to magically appear. Obviously, it's not that simple. (qtd. in Waters, 2015)

Christensen himself has expressed concern about the use of "disruptive innovation" as a tool to "justify whatever anybody—an entrepreneur or a college student—wants to do" (Bennett, 2014; also see Christensen, Raynor, & McDonald, 2015). Likewise, institutions of higher education should be cautious in embracing the mantra of "disruption" as a convenient rationalization for eliminating, transforming, or creating academic programs. Therefore, the degree to which crises are being manufactured to fit the preconceived beliefs and value systems of a few influential individuals is a topic worthy of closer examination in higher education. In recent years, boards of trustees have become increasingly activist in demanding the closure of important academic departments, the implementation of online degrees, the transformation of degree curricula, and the erosion of tenure protections. While such changes may be labeled as "innovative," they are perhaps more accurately described as "impulsive." Such decisions too often fail to consider, for example, how the closure of one academic department can negatively impact the scholarship of an entire college, how a poorly executed online degree program can damage the reputation of the entire university, or how the imposition of a top-down hierarchical structure in a university can drive away supremely talented faculty who cherish autonomy and need job security to test new ideas and drive progress in their respective fields.

Later in this book, we will argue that the judgment of institutional stakeholders is necessary to evaluate, over time, whether or not such changes are truly innovative, in need of refinement, or lack real impact. The growing number of academic programs being preemptively dismantled under the guise of "disruptive innovation" has not received the same level of scholarly scrutiny as the handful of businesses that have actually been displaced by a disruptive technology. Any individual or organization developing a strategy for handling the potential technologies that could disrupt an institution's student intake or revenue stream also should be mindful of the institution's areas of strength, as well as the impact of cuts on the culture of the organization as a whole (Tierney, 1988).

Today, the rhetoric of disruption has become so prevalent that it is almost become a gospel unto itself. One of the most vexing problems we have in higher education today is the reluctance of both administrators and researchers to admit when a particular implementation of technology has failed to effectively convey course content, failed to support the teaching mission of an institution, failed to engage students, and, in essence, failed to be innovative. Administrators are especially loathe to speak openly about the political and financial problems facing their institutions. Instead, they casually sprinkle innocent-sounding words like "accountability," "efficiency," and "innovation" into their public statements while their knowing employees hear phrases like "increased bureaucracy," "resource reallocation," and "layoffs of valuable human capital." Some who openly question the orthodoxy of disruptive innovation are in danger of being dismissed as "luddites" who fail to grasp the extreme challenges confronting contemporary higher education.

Organizations that strive toward Christensen's form of disruption naturally have work patterns entirely different from institutions where longevity and safety are cherished. Therein lies the problem. As we will argue in this book, the accrued expertise offered by longevity can be a vital stimulant to innovation. An individual who feels that their job is safe is more likely to experiment and learn, secure in the notion that they can openly admit failure and learn from past mistakes. Moreover, there are legitimate ideological and empirical concerns with how disruptive innovation has already impacted higher education. These concerns are explained in greater detail below.

Ideological Concerns

To express our ideological concerns with how disruptive innovation is applied to higher education, we will begin with an analysis of how online education has changed the relationship between instructors and institutions—and how this altered relationship impacts the learning environment for students. A generation ago, the notion of the instructor and the class was neither a question nor a concern. A professor developed a syllabus, showed it to a faculty committee, and then taught the class. Odds were good that the professor might change the syllabus a bit for the next year's class, and no one had any concerns. If, after a matter of years, the professor transferred to another university, the syllabus followed along, and perhaps the most disruption the professor faced was figuring out how to cram a semester's worth of reading into the new campus's quarter system. If the course already existed on the new campus—Theories in Sociology, for example—then there was likely not even a committee review of the instructor's syllabus.

Virtual education, in conjunction with learning management systems and quality control frameworks, has changed that scenario not only for those who teach online but also for everyone else. Although many of us have taught large lecture classes, the thought of teaching around the world to thousands of students simultaneously in "real time" would have been ludicrous. Such possibilities raise multiple questions. "The professor's syllabus," as an expression of their professional expertise, is becoming an artifact of the past. The instructor is no longer hermetically sealed within the four walls of a classroom, and instead needs to rely on the tech department to embed videos and create online screens that allow the sorts of interactions that virtual classrooms require.

An unintended consequence, and certainly an example of disruptive behavior, is that when a professor moves to another institution, the question of whether they can take the syllabus suddenly lacks a clear "yes" or "no" answer. Some will argue that the professor cannot take the intellectual property created in one organization to another organization without prior agreement. A corporate university may look at a professor's scrawled handwritten notes for a seminar of a dozen students as trivial, but when that same professor teaches a class of 1,000, the ownership of a syllabus raises new questions in the 21st-century university. Thousands of dollars are at stake.

The result is that teaching becomes a substitution of replaceable parts, and this *milieu* raises what Boaventura de Sousa Santos (2012) calls "strong questions":

> At its best, the modern university has been a locus of free and independent thinking and of the celebration of diversity . . . Bear in mind that for 30 years the tendency to transform the truth value of knowledge has become increasingly strong; [is] there any future for nonconformist, critical, heterodox non-market-able knowledge, and for professors, researchers, and students pursuing it? (9)

Who teaches a class becomes irrelevant, and certainly, the creation of the knowledge for the class is not owned by any one individual. What frames the class, the pedagogy, the instructor, and the institution itself is the market. Teachers are replaceable, and the knowledge that is most valued has little to do with questioning common assumptions or resisting accepted practices. Perhaps most disturbingly, all students are presumed to be receptive to the same syllabus, the same readings, and the same pedagogical practices—no matter their prior experiences with technology or their educational, cultural, or societal backgrounds.

Certainly, such an example is disruptive; however, concerns arise. Academic freedom, tenure, shared governance, and autonomy fall by the wayside, and these are central tenets of higher education that, in Chapter 8, we will argue are vital for individual and organizational innovation.

Academic freedom is circumscribed by technology that can monitor one's words and actions. If professors are replaceable, then tenure is irrelevant. Knowledge is not something one creates but simply an artifact one produces to improve market share. Shared governance, too, is irrelevant because the decisions that need to be made are certainly not improved by collaborative decision making, and, if anything, are slowed down at a time when project implementation needs to be speeded up. The autonomy to test new teaching strategies and trial new readings takes a backseat to consistency between sections and handpicked "best practices" that purportedly illustrate how everyone should engage in online pedagogy, no matter the instructor's areas of expertise or the students' specific skills and needs.

By no means do we wish to romanticize or fetishize the past as if the college or university in the 1950s was the ideal for how knowledge should be produced and disseminated. We also entirely understand the import of change. What we raise here, however, is a concern for disruption that is not simply producing a new way of teaching a class but also eliminating what heretofore had been key precepts not simply of academic life but of institutions that gained notoriety in the 20th century because of a commitment to excellence. Is it not possible that disruption not simply creates a new way of learning but also eliminates that which enables creative inquiry?

We are suggesting that the university is facing a crisis of legitimacy, and—rather than assuming that this crisis is a natural stage as products, goods, and services change—we are asking if these suggested changes are not part and parcel of a neoconservative agenda aimed at stifling academic thought and learning rather than enabling and advancing it? As De Sousa Santos has pointed out, as globalization has taken hold in the university "it meant that its identified institutional weaknesses—and they were many—instead of serving as justification for a vast politico-pedagogical reform program, were declared insurmountable and used to justify the generalized opening of the university-as-public-good to commercial exploitation" (2010, 2). The mercantilization of the university is not simply an extension of what has existed, then, but an entirely new organization—hence, disruptive.

These changes, then, are not nonideological but actually the opposite as they try to place the university squarely within the market. As Sotiris (2014) notes, "it is not enough to theorize commodification and privatization [of the university]. What is needed is to actually try and think of the changing role of the University as a hegemonic apparatus" (5). Our task might even be more ambitious for we are not opponents of innovation. However, we work from the assumption that one must understand not only the tactical strengths (and weaknesses) of the historic college and university but also the strategic character of the current transformations—which include commodification, entrepreneurialization, and privatization—as components of a capitalist hegemony. Do these changes work in a way that is intended in higher education—and elsewhere?

Empirical Concerns

Before we engage with such an analysis, however, we need to turn to our empirical concerns with disruptive innovation theory. Christensen's work was logically built through the power of his argument. Those who resonated with it were less likely to raise the objections we have just entered, and there was very little testing of his hypotheses. Indeed, most of what he did was to present evidence that supported his argument—and his argument was thoughtful, compelling, and logical. The movement from the typewriter to the computer, or from the telegraph to the telephone, had a contemporary resonance that many readers could understand and appreciate. Christensen and his colleagues then worked backward to explain how typewriter companies went out of business and Apple thrived.

The problem with his analysis is that it has not held up to careful analysis. Jill Lepore (2014) in the *New Yorker* offered a devastating critique that outlined why Christensen's theory had multiple shortcomings. She pointed out numerous examples that were the opposite of what Christensen was claiming, as well as examples themselves that *The Innovator's Dilemma* had used that were false. She also cited evidence that companies focused on sustainable, or incremental, technologies are frequently more resilient and prosperous than proponents of disruptive innovation are willing to concede. And then Andrew King and Baljir Baatartogtokh (2015) undertook a thoughtful analysis of Christensen's theory and showed that only seven of the original sample of 77 disruptive innovations first cited by Christensen and Raynor (2003) correspond to the theory. Hence, they pointed out, "despite the theory's widespread use and appeal, its essential validity and generalizability have been seldom tested in the academic literature" (78). In their subsequent analysis, they faulted the idea for problematic assumptions that did not hold up to rigorous testing and measurement. Although the ideas were of some utility, the internal organizational conditions and the complexity of environmental conditions had them conclude "the threats faced by the companies in our sample were deeply challenging and they cannot be understood from a single viewpoint" (85).

Two Recent Examples of
Failed "Disruptions" in Higher Education

1. For-Profit Colleges and Universities

One example of a more radical approach to innovation, and an organization that apparently is facile enough to innovate on a moment's notice, has been the for-profit sector. Curious to us, and to critics and boosters alike, FPCUs have been thought to be among the most innovative of postsecondary institutions; nonetheless, these are precisely the sort of institutions that experienced the greatest decline in the last decade—and most level-headed analysts would say that their decline is of their own doing. The argument for their ability to innovate is that they could scale up and down based on market demand. If customers needed courses in computer technology, then a for-profit would find a classroom and instructor to teach the class at a time and place that is convenient. When customers no longer needed those courses and instead wanted instruction in graphic design, then the organization would simply let the comp tech instructor go and instead hire an instructor versed in graphic design. The lethargic pace of decision making in traditional institutions was eliminated; the forced labor costs of tenure-track faculty was not an issue since instructors were part-time and contingent. For-profits were viewed as models of innovative organizations that traditional institutions ought to emulate. A great many of the characteristics that Christensen pointed out in his disruptive model resonated with those of us who were tracking FPCUs (Tierney & Hentschke, 2007). For-profit higher education had grown from a blip on the screen to 12% of the entire industry. And technology and social media were forcing changes in industries that had long been seen as solid—newspapers, department stores, travel agencies, and the like. The University of Phoenix became the largest university in the country. For-profit higher education was the wave of the future!

Until it wasn't. The result was not simply that federal and state governments sought to close down many for-profits that were acting in bad faith, but, perhaps more importantly, the consumers in a market-driven environment soured on the for-profit industry. By the start of the 21st century, for-profit higher education came under attack for scurrilous business practices. It turns out that students in too many of the for-profits neither learned very much nor graduated with viable job prospects. Students accumulated a mountain of debt. Even without sufficient government oversight, consumers began to recognize the for-profit industry as a lemon (Shireman, 2018a). It is hard not to conclude that the for-profits hurt themselves through avarice and an inability to accept responsibility. Ultimately, the dramatic increase in for-profit higher education was followed by just as dramatic a contraction.

Ironically, successful for-profit institutions were the ones that were least likely to innovate in a manner that required enormous growth year after year. Instead, they offered the customer a relatively traditional experience, albeit usually not on a traditional campus or with tenured faculty. In retrospect, higher education is indeed in deep trouble if a goldrush mentality is necessary for survival. If innovations foster exploitation, then not only colleges and universities—but the students who need an education and the country that needs an educated workforce—should be worried.

2. Massive Open Online Courses, or MOOCs

A second sort of disruptive innovation also has yet to attain the promise it once held. MOOCs—massive open on-line courses—were also touted as the online behemoth that was going to force postsecondary closures at a rate that would have made Drucker and Christensen true prophets. In 2011, when Sebastian Thrun, a professor of computer science at Stanford University, uploaded the same introductory lectures on artificial intelligence he provided to students paying $52,000 a year in Palo Alto, MOOCs certainly appeared to be the future of higher education.[9] An estimated 160,000 people viewed his engaging broadcasts within three months, and Thrun gave up his tenured position at Stanford to become a Google Fellow, helping to establish the first private educational company devoted to the development of MOOCs: Udacity (Chafkin, 2013; Konnikova, 2014). Udacity, Coursera, and other MOOCs accumulated a great deal of venture capital with the expectation that enormous sums of money were to be made. Seminars would have not 10, 100, or even 1,000 students but instead attract consumers from throughout the world. Declaring that MOOCs were inaugurating "a budding revolution in global online higher education," the *New York Times* commentator and best-selling author Thomas Friedman breathlessly exclaimed the following in 2013:

Nothing has more potential to lift more people out of poverty—by providing them an affordable education to get a job or improve in the job they have. Nothing has more potential to unlock a billion more brains to solve the world's biggest problems. And nothing has more potential to enable us to reimagine higher education than the massive open online course, or MOOC (Friedman, 2013).

Others claimed that traditional colleges and universities were about to be swamped by the MOOC tidal wave. Anant Agarwal, president of edX, a MOOC jointly developed by MIT and Harvard, shared that 155,000 students from various countries throughout the world took the first class, an introduction to circuitry, offered by edX. With no small degree of pride, he pointed out that number was "greater than the total number of MIT alumni in its 150-year history" (Friedman, 2013). The future was MOOCs!

Except it wasn't. MOOCs were one of the most covered topics in higher education less than 10 years ago, and today they are beset with problems and a massive lowering of expectations. No one ever figured out the business model that might enable MOOCs to take off. The completion rates for MOOCs were abysmal; one 2013 study of 17 Coursera classes indicated that only 5% of enrolled students finished their coursework (Perna et al., 2013). Perhaps even worse, MOOCs were shown to promote poor habits among students, such as passive learning and an inability to apply knowledge once it had been learned. One UK researcher who studied a MOOC offered by Harvard Medical School stated the following:

> Learners focused on activities such as watching videos and taking tests, with little evidence of learning relating new knowledge into practice, or of connecting to their peers through the discussion board. To be effective, professional learning should provide opportunities to integrate theoretical and practical knowledge. But even those learners who said they wanted to improve their professional practice did not integrate the scientific knowledge they learned through the MOOC with practical, on-the-job learning.[10]

An equity issue concerning MOOCs was discovered rather early in their development, as well. The small percentage of students who were enrolling and completing MOOCs were largely young, well-educated, and employed people who were autodidacts looking to enhance existing skills (Christensen et al., 2013). In short, they were the types of individuals who frequented the libraries of previous generations. Moreover, the technology is still not optimal, especially in rural environments and developing countries—a problem that undercuts the once widespread belief that MOOCs could "democratize" education. And when a MOOC lecturer does not have the deep content knowledge and magnetic personality of a Sebastian Thrun, the content gets criticized for not being engaging. As Kim and Maloney (2020) have wisely observed, "MOOCs violated almost every core principle of active learning with which quality online and blended courses were designed" (143). Instead of being learner centered and recognizing the diversity of learners in higher education, MOOCs were focused primarily on content delivery and the publicity associated with superstar professors like Thrun.

Innovations, by definition, are experiments, and experiments sometimes fail. But as an innovation, MOOCs were not a useful guide for those of us in higher education in terms of how to reshape and rethink our organizations. If MOOCs had been successful, they may well have given traditional higher education a run for its money. One challenge of disruption theory is that we often look at successful disruption: computers put typewriters out of business, telephones supplanted the telegraph, and so on. Aside from serious questions about the applicability of profit-making theories in a nonprofit world, we also must recognize that, for every successful innovator, there are numerous others whose bright ideas fail.

Concluding Thoughts

Although Christensen's acolytes, such as Michael Horn (2018, 2019), forecast a more nuanced future, it is difficult not to come away from research pertaining to disruption and innovation with the feeling that the academic sky is falling. When prophets claim "the end is near," dire change is needed—and it is needed immediately. Sinners who preach the values of circumspection and deliberation need to repent. What do those of us in higher education need to do? Apparently, innovate! And innovation means, basically, "out with the old; in with the new." Such a vision of innovation is grounded in uniquely American beliefs that innovation equals radical change. Disruptive innovations are designed to capture the attention of Rogers's (2003) famous "early adopters" who have the agency, explicit skills, wealth, and time to understand a new innovation and make effective use of it. According to disruptive innovation theory, individuals who lack these specific traits may be excluded from participation until the innovation is simplified, affordable, and made more accessible. For students and faculty endeavoring to make higher education work in the present, though, exuberance about impeding disruption is not enough. Strategic planning and consideration of the people who might be most negatively impacted—and even pushed out of higher education—is necessary.

The result is that we are left with the following issues. We acknowledge that student debt, the negative public perception of higher education, and demographic and institutional instabilities could herald a fractured system of higher education. We also recognize that today's postsecondary learners are different from yesterday's—and this fact indicates that substantive change to higher education is necessary.

While we agree that innovation needs to be a key factor for universities of the future, we nevertheless have deep concerns about the ideological and empirical justifications for disruptive innovation as a theory. We have also seen that, within the sector of higher education, for-profit institutions and MOOCs have failed to live up to the promises of disruption. So, where do we go from here?

Research from Christensen's colleagues at Harvard Business School may point to one useful direction. For years, Germany—not the United States—has been identified by Harvard Business School and the World Economic Forum as the most prolific country in terms of innovation (Breznitz, 2014; Schwab, 2018). However, Germany's preferred path to innovation is more measured, more socially responsible. In short, Germany considers the impact of innovation on a variety of constituencies, projects the impact of innovations on a long-term basis, and has a healthy respect for incremental innovations that may not seem exciting from an entrepreneurial perspective but may be more viable and helpful from an institutional perspective. Such a process is known in Europe as "responsible innovation," and it serves as a useful model for our own work. We agree with numerous aspects of the "Responsible Research and Innovation" initiative of the European Union's Framework Programs, including their emphasis on societal challenges, high ethical standards, respect for the environment, and attentiveness to diverse perspectives, including gender equity in scientific disciplines (Smallman, 2018; Stilgoe, Owen, & Macnaghten, 2013). We also agree with theorists who have emphasized the importance of reflection and deliberation in the creative process, as well as responsiveness to various communities who might be impacted by an innovative process or product (Owen, Bessant, & Heintz, 2013).

It is worth noting that German companies also invest heavily in research and development, to the tune of 80 billion Euros, through its university sector and other public institutions (Goethe Institute, 2015; Schoeman, 2016). In fact, the Fraunhofer Institutes, which are concurrently financed through public monies and private investment, are compared favorably to venerable innovative U.S. institutions like Bell Labs in that they welcome interdisciplinary approaches to applied research while demonstrating an admirable tolerance for trial and error (Breznitz, 2014; Comin, 2016; Gertner, 2012). Some elements of the German economy, which has far more government coordination and a greater reliance on small- to medium-sized businesses than the liberal market economy of the United States, are nearly impossible to reproduce without wholesale philosophical and political change (Lanford & Maruco, 2018, 2019). However, the German attitude toward innovations is quite replicable if higher education institutions make a concerted effort to focus on long-term investment and societal impact rather than the potential for short-term windfall and disruption. Such an approach is much closer to the "mindful innovation" that we espouse for higher education in this book.

Our rebuttal to disruptive innovation, then, is fourfold. First, a deeper conceptualization of innovation is needed for higher education than the current definitions that exist for businesses and corporations. Second, individuals need to be given the opportunity to employ their talents and developed skills in service of creative and innovative inquiry. Third, a deliberate culture of mindful innovation needs to be stimulated within our higher education institutions that is less focused on efficiency and more focused on empowerment. Fourth, the factors that promote mindful innovation are identifiable and protected by four tenets of traditional academic life—academic freedom, tenure, shared governance, and institutional autonomy—that are unfortunately under attack in contemporary discourse on higher education. In the next chapter, we will draw a distinction between our vision for higher education and how higher education's problems have been analyzed through the value systems of neoliberalism and New Public Management. We will then present our conceptualization of mindful innovation, along with our understanding of related terms such as "creativity" and "entrepreneurship."

Chapter 4

How Higher Education's Problems
Have Been Analyzed

Introduction

Many of the solutions that innovation proponents have put forward are based on strikingly similar analyses of the problems. Michael Horn (2018), for example, or economists such as Richard Vedder (2017), commonly point to the fixed costs of higher education as the culprit. If colleges and universities were nimble, they might be able to adapt to the marketplace—like for-profits. Starbucks, for instance, added pastries and then luncheon foods to their shops and were remarkably successful. But when the wine and beer experiment did not succeed, it simply closed that part of the enterprise. Starbucks can add and subtract workers without undo hassles if an innovation fails. Such an analysis underscores why there was so much enthusiasm for the for-profit institutions and MOOCs.

Tenure: The Cause of "Baumol's Disease?"

The culprit for academe's fixed costs largely rests on the structure of tenure. In both academic writings and the popular media, tenure has been identified as the cause of "Baumol's disease" in secondary and higher education environments (Bowen, 2012; Brewer & Tierney, 2012; Hill & Roza, 2010; Worstall, 2011). In the 1960s, economist William Baumol pointed out that labor-intensive industries face problems if they wish to change or increase output because of fixed staffing. His best example pertained to a string quartet. By definition, a string quartet needs four musicians, and, as they gain experience, their salaries and related costs rise. Since the concert hall has a set number of seats, management must ensure that the hall sells out for every concert, and the cost of the tickets will need to rise to meet the increase in costs. As the cost of tickets rise, some concert-goers will refrain from attending. Costs rise, and revenue decreases (Baumol & Bowen, 1966).

To many students of disruption, tenure is a central perpetrator of the problems academe faces because of Baumol's disease. Indeed, the structure of tenure creates an organizational culture with far too many fixed costs. When a significant component of the organization is guaranteed job security, then other actors seek similar protections. At one point, colleges and universities had more full-time workers than part-timers, and full-timers earned benefits such as health care and other subsidies. Many in academe began to think if colleges and universities could reduce their fixed costs, they not only would be financially better off but would also be more innovative. Tenure, the argument went, created a cadre of workers who were against change—especially technological change that could improve labor productivity—and dedicated to the status quo.

The claim that tenure is the cause of academe's woes, however, has three problems and two outcomes. We will address the problems first. The first problem concerns faculty salaries. Instructional salaries represent, across 2- and 4-year institutions, less than one-third of the total expenditures for all public colleges and universities (Barnshaw & Dunietz, 2015). Contrary to the beliefs of many observers of higher education, faculty benefits in the form of medical, dental, retirement, and other forms of compensation also have been shown not to contribute to higher tuition costs (Barnshaw & Dunietz, 2015). Moreover, over the last 50 years, we have seen a steady erosion in the total number of tenured and tenure-track faculty, with no corresponding decline in tuition expenses. In fact, during one of the most rapid periods of tuition increases—2002 to 2013—Rhoades and Frye (2015) conclusively demonstrated that all sectors of higher education experienced stark reductions in (1) the overall number of tenured and tenure-track faculty, (2) the salary outlays for full-time faculty per full-time students, and (3) the total instructional salaries and wages as a share of total education and general expenditures. The authors conclude their executive report with the following statement:

In short, academic labor costs are not driving tuition increases. The trend lines run in opposite directions. Relative academic labor costs have gone down as tuition has gone up. Students are paying more to go to colleges that are spending less on instruction. (3)

A longitudinal perspective can be helpful here. As Table 4.1 illustrates, higher education has become extraordinarily reliant on contingent labor over the past 50 years. Compared with the days (e.g., 1969) in which the tuition and fees associated with higher education were negligible (and, in some cases, nonexistent), tenured and tenure-track faculty today constitute a minimal proportion of the total professoriate.

It is worth noting here that the average salary for part-time faculty working at a single institution during the 2016–2017 academic year was $20,508 (Shulman et al., 2017), and only 5% of higher education institutions offer medical or retirement benefits to part-time instructors (Harmon et al., 2018). Due to this accumulation of evidence, we are hard pressed to say that tenure is a structure that contributes to the exorbitant increases in student tuition the United States has experienced in recent generations—or prevents innovation from taking root in higher education. Indeed, those institutions that critics claim are the least innovative are also the ones that have low cadres of tenured faculty.

The second problem is that the movement away from tenure-track positions in academe also has resulted in a movement toward outsourcing other components of the organization (Wekullo, 2017). If a privileged group loses job protections, it stands to reason that other groups will as well. Consequently, those who are the lowest paid also are no longer seen as fixed costs—they can be outsourced for cheaper labor. Recognize, of course, that those who are on the lowest economic rung also account for the least amount of fixed costs. Colleges and universities have increased outsourcing

Table 4.1. Proportion of Tenure-Track Faculty in 1969, 2009, and 2016

	Non-Tenure Track	Tenure Track
1969	21.7%	78.3%
2009	66.5%	33.5%
2016	73.0%	27.0%

Sources: Adrianna Kezar and Daniel Maxey, "The Changing Academic Workforce" and AAUP, "Data Snapshot: Contingent Faculty in U.S. Higher Ed."

to cut costs by a considerable amount, presumably to increase the environment for innovation. Such reasoning has been traced to C.K. Prahalad and Gary Hamel's (1990) influential and clever conceptualization of "core competencies," those essential activities through which a company not only maintains industry relevance but asserts its competitive advantages. When Prahalad and Hamel first advanced their concept of core competencies in the pages of *Harvard Business Review*, they never imagined that efficiency-minded managers might extend their idea by outsourcing every activity that did not directly and clearly feed into a core competency. Nevertheless, "strategic outsourcing" quickly became as much a part of the business literature as "core competencies" (e.g., Quinn & Hilmer, 1994), and one need only look at the involvement of for-profit food service companies like Aramark or dormitory operators like Corvias Property Management to see how the ideas behind outsourcing have resonated in higher education. After all, if a service is not central to the mission and identity of an institution, why should a college or university expend considerable resources to support it?

One rebuttal against outsourcing that is related to the mission of higher education would concern *equity*. These outsourcing arrangements rarely improve wages for marginalized workers in food service and institutional support capacities, and they generally lack health benefits. An additional rebuttal would concern the inevitable conflicts of interest that arise when the fundamental mission of *teaching and learning*, not to mention *student safety*, works against a for-profit entity's bottom line. A distressing example of these conflicts occurred during the height of the Covid-19 pandemic. In May 2020, Corvias Property Management sent a warning letter to their partner, the University System of Georgia Board of Regents (U.S.), that limitations on the capacity of dormitories in an effort to implement social distancing and reduce the spread of Covid-19 could not be implemented in a unilateral fashion (Marcus, 2021). The management company further threatened that any reductions in dormitory capacity, discounts in student fees, or plans to discourage students from living on campus in the Fall of 2020—no matter how important such measures were for student safety and overall campus health—would violate the contract between Corvias and the Georgia Board of Regents (Williams, 2020). In recent years, colleges and universities have sought to outsource entire degree programs with for-profit companies like Noodle (Marcus, 2021), and it is fair to wonder how quickly such arrangements will also contravene educational missions related to equity, teaching and learning, and safety.

A final rebuttal to outsourcing would recognize that *organizational creativity* relies on diverse perspectives and creative conflict for the development and implementation of an *innovation*. In other words, it is imprudent to assume that a small handful of departments constitute the "core competencies" of an educational institution, particularly when innovation is a goal of the organization (Hoecht & Trott, 2006). Organizational creativity is enhanced by input from multiple disciplines, programs, and perspectives, and colleges and universities are in danger of relinquishing one of their major advantages—the multiplicity of human experience—when they outsource seemingly peripheral activities. This is a major concern pertinent to our discussion, and we will return to it in subsequent chapters.

The third problem is that the treatment of tenure as a fixed cost that needs to be eliminated does not take into consideration the benefits of tenure to innovation. In later chapters we will demonstrate that years of empirical research points to autonomy, creative conflict, diversity, and intrinsic motivation as factors that have a positive impact on innovative thinking, production, and implementation. Without tenure, researchers and instructors are less likely to feel they have the autonomy to test ideas that are likely to fail numerous times before a truly innovative process or product takes shape. Without tenure, professors are more likely to chase grants out of a desire to prove their economic value to the institution, rather than pursue a research agenda inspired by intrinsic motivation. Without tenure, creative conflict and critical inquiry will suffer because researchers and instructors will be concerned about alienating colleagues who might determine the future of their employment. Additionally, without tenure, it is unlikely that individuals from diverse backgrounds would feel comfortable engaging in spirited debate, especially with individuals who hold a higher rank within the organization. Research has also demonstrated that faculty hiring practices are likely to be less diverse when individuals do not have the job security to engage in open and honest dialogue about the exclusionary practices and histories of their institutions (e.g., Gonzales et al., 2021; Liera, 2020).

Those who mistakenly lament the costs of tenure also fail to take into account the benefits of tenure not only to the individual but to the organization. No one suggests that a string quartet should be downsized to a trio. The quality of the music would not only be diminished but substantively different. One might suggest that technology could replace musicians, but the timbre of the music would be altered tremendously, the humanistic aspect to any live performance would be completely removed, and the expertise of the musicians, along with their ability to produce a unique interpretation of composer's music, would be sorely missed.

Similarly, the raison d'etre of academic life is not to insipidly reiterate notes on a page; rather, it is the pursuit of truth in the classroom and in one's research, grounded in years of accrued expertise, the development of new theories, and no small amount of contemplation and deep reading. The idea commonly known as academic freedom came about in the United States in the early 20th century. Many will argue academic freedom is the central component that made U.S. universities among the best in the world. Academic freedom exists not through the goodwill of anyone but because the structure of tenure was created to protect it. To cast aside tenure based on dubious reasoning is also to cast aside the idea of academic freedom. It is curious reasoning to suggest that when a structure that existed to protect an idea is eliminated that the idea remains. The result is that the diminution of tenure also has weakened a central totem of the academy.

Two Cultural Outcomes of Tenure's Demise

The outcomes of tenure's demise in higher education can be best viewed through a cultural lens. First, tenure came about to protect academic freedom so that individuals might search for truth. The assumption was that one ought to be able to follow one's ideas wherever they may take them. The ideal case was to point out that external interferences were not to intrude on one's work. Faculty also had the right to speak up about the governance of the institution. We are well aware of the flaws that can be pointed out, and we appreciate the challenges that tenure generates and have written about them (Tierney & Lanford, 2014). Certainly, some faculty used tenure as job security and little more. Shared governance has often slowed down decision making.

But what critics of tenure fail to consider is what has been lost in terms of research and development, how an institutional culture conducive to creative exploration has been changed and eroded, and how the lack of shared decision making has resulted in decisions that frequently cut against the grain of what academic life can contribute through innovative inquiry. At the same time, the diminishment of academic freedom has empowered a managerial class that consolidates authority and exponentially intensifies faculty surveillance through a variety of questionable metrics while growing administrative salaries and benefits far beyond anything that the majority of faculty enjoy (Erickson, Hanna, & Walker, 2021; Krupnick & Marcus, 2015; Oleksiyenko, 2018).

We are suggesting that, when one thinks about innovation, we not only need to consider the presumed benefits of change but also what the ancillary costs will be to the culture of the organization. We are reminded of the famous comment reported by *New York Times* journalist Peter Arnett during the Vietnam War in which a U.S. major justified the bombing of the South Vietnamese town of Bén Tre by saying, "It became necessary to destroy the town to save it" (Arnett, 1968). We certainly do not want to overstate the analogy, but there are many innovation gurus who seek to destroy higher education to presumably save it. What we have endeavored to point out is that their solutions have not panned out. Even worse, they are repeatedly based on incorrect assumptions and data.

The second outcome is that education gets reduced to a commodity that is traded on the market. Until recently, higher education was never simply a private good that benefited the individual. The assumption was that a postsecondary degree not only increased the wages of the graduate but also aided the country. The arguments put forward by the standard innovators, however, have little to do with the advancement and well-being of the citizenry. We have seen the salaries of academe's senior management rise because they are ostensibly doing more important work—they are the innovators. The result is that wage discrepancy between the highest and lowest paid in an institution has never been greater. Again, one needs to ask if the environment we are creating through such innovations is the culture that will enable the mission we desire for higher education.

The Impact of Neoliberalism and New Public Management on Higher Education

Unfortunately, arguments over the importance of innovation in higher education are often met with such resistance that the groups end up talking past one another. In one group are those who claim that the end is near. In another group are individuals who rebut or smirk at the underlying themes that innovation's proponents put forward; however, they have few suggestions about how to handle the fundamental problems that currently beset academe and require immediate action.

Those who have the most trouble with contemporary changes in academe work largely from a critique of neoliberalism and what has come to be called New Public Management (NPM) (Hood, 1995). Neoliberalism, argue the critics, shifted the notion of education as a public good into discourse about markets, institutional and individual competition, and self-interest (Naidoo & Williams, 2015). We need not go into a full exegesis of the roots of neoliberalism through the writings of the Anglo-Austrian social theorist and political philosopher Friedrich von Hayek and the American economist Milton Friedman, but the underlying tenets of neoliberalism are important to understand for those who critique the current mania about disruption and innovation in higher education. At its core, neoliberalism stands for the renaissance in laissez-faire economic thought that casts a critical eye toward governmental intervention, labor unions, taxation, and other activities that may be perceived as infringements upon individual choice. As described by Shahjahan and Hill (2019), one way to view neoliberalism is through a "set of macro market driven developments such as marketization, privatization, consumerism, and a human capital development emphasis" (para. 1). The neoliberal assumption is not so much that what was formerly known as public goods are necessarily bad but that they should not be subsidized by the public.

Some will argue that the public good in question might be useful and necessary, but it is a "bad" public good (Shaw, 2010) because it does not achieve its goals and can be done more cheaply by others. The rise of charter schools was partially based on the notion that, for a variety of reasons, schools were not adequately educating students. Why not spend public monies on private providers who can either do a better job or do the job less expensively, thereby saving the public sector money? The same sort of logic is what prompted postsecondary institutions to outsource various tasks. From this perspective, public education is a public good, but those who clean the buildings where public education takes place are irrelevant. If the task is simply to clean buildings, and a private company can do the task more cheaply, why not outsource the work? The task is important, but a decision about who should ultimately accomplish the task is made strictly on financial considerations.

The critique of neoliberalism is that all such actions are ideological, and the idea of outsourcing, or finding providers who can undertake tasks more cheaply is, or ought to be, the defining characteristic of human relations. From this vantage point, obviously students are customers—they are paying for a product just like individuals who buy groceries from a supermarket. Shoppers have comparable and varying preferences. Shoppers who go to a grocery store, buy tainted food, and fall ill will no longer go to that store.

Some shoppers prefer quality products and do not mind paying extra for the product; others simply want what is quickest or cheapest. Similarly, a college that does not adequately educate a student for a job will not attract students. Some will want the traditional college experience with a campus and dormitories; others will want what is most convenient. The market decides what is right.

The result is that efficiency and effectiveness are prioritized. Taxes should be low because the best way to achieve the task is through the market. Unions, collective bargaining agreements, and the like distort the market because they do not pay the workers what they are worth based on market value. Instead, individuals enter into agreements that have little to do with market priorities. Markets ensure that people get what they deserve—or merit. Merit is fetishized such that individuals earn what they have created and no one has undo advantage. If one does not succeed, it is the individual's fault, and society deserves little, if any, blame. The fewer regulations, the better, because ultimately the market will determine success. Yes, a few people may get ill from buying tainted meat, but ultimately that shop will go out of business. And the cost of regulating companies ultimately is more harmful to society than unfettered competition because regulation stifles true competition. The world gets defined by competition, and ultimately there will be winners and losers. A critic of neoliberalism, Chris Lorenz (2012), is worth quoting at length here:

> Neoliberalism simultaneously shifts its focus from rights to risks; it represents "risk society," job insecurity, and "flexibility" to be the normal, present-day "global" condition. Neoliberalism thus silently uncouples the globalized individual from fundamental rights formerly connected to national citizenship, like the right to schooling and welfare. It trades all these civil rights for one new right: the right to buy services on the privatized service market. (602)

Hamer and Lang (2015) take this analysis one step further and speak of the structural violence of neoliberalism that increases racism for people of color who work within higher education. And too, recognize how those who say that colleges and universities must innovate or face closure fall into this thinking. Innovation, from this perspective, is part and parcel of the neoliberal ideology. What once was public and nonprofit now needs to be made private and more competitive. Competition defines all activity.

Efficiency and effectiveness get described in a particular manner. Every task and outcome needs to be evaluated in a manner than enables comparison. Many will point out how higher education has been in the grip of neoliberalism for 2 decades. Rankings, international competition, education hubs, the rise of for-profits, the decrease in funding of public goods, the constant review and analysis of a faculty member's and department's productivity are all primary levers to implement market rationales on a previous public good (Altbach & Hazelkorn, 2017; Knight, 2018; Lanford & Tierney, 2016; Oleksiyenko & Tierney, 2018; Pusser & Marginson, 2013).

What has come to be known as New Public Management (NPM) is the instrument that implements neoliberalism (Lorenz, 2012). NPM assumes that the way to improve public service is to use management practices from the private sector. Most often, what gets mentioned is a disdain for collective bargaining and the assumption that all users are customers. What often gets overlooked, especially in postsecondary education, is the transformed role of upper management and Boards of Trustees. Those who are most handsomely rewarded in the private sector are the CEOs; boards function to improve profitability. The result is that college presidents have seen their salaries rise while other salaries have remained flat or are outsourced. As nonprofit entities, university boards cannot claim profits and salaries. However, they can claim perks and preferences, their increased oversight is seen as normal, and shared governance is viewed as an outmoded model unable to make efficient decisions.

Although NPM superficially appears to be a neutral approach to good management, critics see NPM as anything but neutral (e.g., Deem and Brehony, 2005). As Lynch (2015) states, "It emphasizes the language of choice, competition, and service users. . . . The new effect is that meeting financial and other targets is a priority" (194). The point is not only to focus on what gets emphasized, but also on what gets deemphasized, such as academic freedom, tenure, shared governance, and the value of activities that cannot be, in the words of Lynch (2015), "measured numerically, hierarchically ordered, and incontrovertibly judged" (190). The assumption of neoliberalism, of course, is that budgets can perpetually be cut, funding can be reduced, and the obligations of the citizenry through taxation and civic action will be lessened. Dent and Barry (2017) have nicely collapsed NPM into six processes that underscore how it is in sync with a neoliberal focus: (1) increasing the breakup of public sector organizations into separately managed units, (2) increasing competition to use management techniques from the private sector, (3) increasing emphasis on discipline and sparing use of resources, (4) more hands-on management, (5) the introduction of measurable indicators of performance, and (6) the use of predetermined standards to measure output (also see Lorenz, 2012, 638).

A great number of analyses have pointed out the impact of neoliberal philosophies and NPM on early career and senior academics (e.g., Darder, 2012; Gonzales, Martinez, & Ordu, 2014; Jubas, 2012; Lawless & Chen, 2017; Levin & Aliyeva, 2015; Osei-Kofi, 2012). Rather than spend time on academic activities or engagement in work aimed at social reform, the academic is judged on neoliberal criteria focused on advancing a privatized agenda. Those who are unable or unwilling to be entrepreneurial are harshly penalized, sometimes with a loss of employment. Creativity gets defined through an economic prism; it is assumed that individuals who are the most creative will be financially rewarded for their work, insofar as that is how the marketplace values excellence. The neoliberal university may begrudgingly recognize that the humanities cannot garner the revenue of their counterparts in engineering and the sciences, so managers will reward humanists with a speaker series and the like. Nevertheless, the bulk of university resources will be for those who are "entrepreneurial" or "innovative," as defined by the ability to generate revenue. Salary inequity between faculty in the sciences and engineering and their counterparts in the humanities has never been greater. Obviously, when the criteria for excellence is based on the ability to generate external funding, the neuroscientist will earn more than twice as much as the poet. To the extent that the university can create an innovative culture that advances entrepreneurial activities, any other activity is seen as superfluous, marginal, or even detrimental.

Arguing against neoliberalism and NPM can be difficult. When a proponent of NPM claims to merely desire "efficiency" or "effectiveness," critics who merely desire a more nuanced discussion can be placed in the awkward position of speaking against efficiency and for inefficiency. To speak for efficiency is to simply point out that time has a value, and the extent to which goods an organization holds can be produced, sold, and used more efficiently is ultimately beneficial for the customer and the business. How can one argue with the idea that winners should be decided based on the idea of merit? Indeed, merit tests came about in the early 20th century to ensure that some students were not discriminated against. The assumption was that an objective test can determine who merits admission. Why should merit not be employed today? Similarly, any objections vocalized against rankings makes one appear that they are for mediocrity. Why would an institution not desire to be "better" than one's competitor? Standardization is good because one's output can be measured against others, and the potential for mass production exists, which in turn, generates revenue and greater efficiencies.

The brilliance of those who support NPM is the rationalization of privatization as an obvious corrective that simply aims to improve education. Who can be against a system where the goal is to better prepare students for gainful employment? Why would anyone object to the university' president raising capital to build a building or create scholarships to attract different sorts of students to the campus?

Obviously, into this discourse enters a concern for innovation. Change, rather than stasis, is not simply what is desired but needed. To be said to be "creative" or "innovative" is generally seen as a compliment in one's teaching and research. To suggest that one is neither creative nor innovative is an insult, and potentially injurious to one's career.

Before the pandemic, however, a spate of articles working against neoliberalism began to criticize the fetishization of innovation. David Sax (2018), in a *New York Times* editorial entitled "End the Innovation Obsession," has claimed that those who focus on innovation can be truly destructive and harmful to learning. Lee Vinsel (2018) has raised important questions about fads like design thinking being "pushed . . . as a reform for all of higher education" when, in actuality, they may be a " 'movement' that's little more than floating balloons of jargon." John Patrick Leary (2018) has documented the wasted resources and inflated rhetoric surrounding innovation initiatives at his own institution, asking "What evidence is there that any of this very expensive innovation and entrepreneurship stuff works—that is, rewards students with fulfilling, well-compensated careers, while generating revenue for the institution (not to mention 'changing the world')?" Henry Giroux (2015), the intellectual fountainhead for critical educational theory, has bemoaned how administrators focus on anti-intellectual change rather than promoting the democratic public sphere. The result is that those who critique neoliberalism and NPM offer a largely trenchant critique of innovation. They implore individuals not only to understand the underpinnings of rhetoric concerning innovation but also to point out how such rhetoric can work in favor of conformity and against innovative thinking. The goal is to work toward a notion of learning and research that produces critical citizenship and scholarship.

We appreciate the critiques that have been made of neoliberalism. Although most proponents of innovation do not make a frontal assault on the core values of academic life, they nevertheless have moved the discussion in a manner that threatens those most important beliefs, as well as the structures that support them. As we have established in the previous chapter, the changes championed by many proponents of innovation have either not yielded significant results, or they have been marginal. It is odd to suggest, for example, that the for-profit industry is a model for innovation, when, at the same time, it has embarrassing rates of bankruptcy, fraud, and criminal complaints. It is equally strange to praise derivatives as a beacon of disruptive innovation (and dismiss legitimate criticism, as Alan Greenspan did) when the societal effects are unclear.

At the same time, the arguments that most neoliberals make are more philosophical than practical. The sorts of issues we raised with regard to the critique of neoliberalism and NPM need to be made, especially in the public sphere. Public intellectuals need to make the case in legislatures and to the broader public about the import of public goods; they also need to describe how a democratic notion of higher education is necessary to ensure funding that enables success in our colleges and universities (Lanford & Tierney, 2018). By coming to grips with the pervasive ways in which neoliberalism and NPM affect daily life, decisions can be put forward that help colleges and universities achieve tangible, clear goals, thus enabling success in the classroom and in the research laboratory.

However, we have argued that the flaws of neoliberalism prevent us from effectively cultivating an innovative environment and, in turn, resolving the many pressing and immediate problems that higher education faces. The college or university that faces a budget deficit, or a continued slide in enrollment, cannot reverse its troubles simply through vociferous critiques of neoliberalism, however elegant or intellectually persuasive. Innovation, as we have defined the idea in this book, is necessary. Simply relying on the ways of the past is not a sufficient guide to the future, which is why in the pages that follow we will advance a vision for mindful innovation.

Chapter 5

Conceptualizing Innovation, Creativity, and Entrepreneurship

An Introduction to Innovation

In 2015, Janet Napolitano, the current president of the University of California system, gave the annual Pullias Lecture at the University of Southern California. The transcript of her speech, entitled "A Trifecta for the Future: Higher Education, California, and Innovation," can be found here.[1] Napolitano made a positive impression amongst much of the audience with her commanding stage presence and impressive ability to convey a message directly and succinctly. In particular, she made a rather pointed message toward the end of her lecture:

> Let's get real.
> California is never going to be a smokestack state.
> It is never going to be a call center state.
> It is never going to be a warehouse state.
> California, if it is to pay its dream forward to future generations, must never abandon its sense of itself as a society built on innovation, and it must never abandon the institutions that seed that innovation. California the Innovation State is the California those who followed the 49ers set out to build, and it is the California their successors fostered across the ensuing generations. That California is the California we are fighting for.

Naturally, such a message is crafted to play well to its audience. Many would argue that the raison d'être of a research university like the University of Southern California is to stimulate innovation among local industries, encourage students to think in innovative ways, and to produce innovative research. The University of Southern California is particularly fixated on innovation, as evidenced by the Stevens Center for Innovation,[2] the Annenberg Innovation Lab,[3] the Viterbi Student Institute for Innovation,[4] and the Jimmy Iovine and Andre Young Academy to encourage Arts, Technology, and the Business of Innovation.[5]

In short, the lecture hall was full of people who like to believe that they are innovative—and who love to believe that their innovative work is central to the success of California.

The sincerity of Napolitano's message is worthy of deeper consideration. Outside of the research university, the notion of a state being defined by innovation is quite appealing for a number of reasons. It conjures notions of a vibrant and educated workforce. It also implies that a state's industries are able to adapt to global trends and changing economic conditions. California certainly has its share of factories, warehouses, and call centers, but the prevailing business-related image that pops into many people's minds is that of Silicon Valley, a location where innovation is perhaps the most valued of commodities.

Therefore, innovation—as a "term" and (for many people) as an "ethos"—is nearly everywhere in contemporary life, as well as in higher education. Its use is not only ubiquitous in corporate boardrooms but also in the coursework of schools of business and management. Media and publicity outlets hired by organizations as different as Google and Harvard University trumpet the most novel technological breakthroughs as evidence of an institution's commitment to innovation—and, presumably, in turn "excellence." We intuitively understand that the "ethos" of innovation is one where new ideas are celebrated, the potential for societal change is great, and a significant amount of financial capital could reward the innovators who have made a positive change in people's lives.

And yet, the "concept" of innovation defies simple explanation. The field of education is a useful example, as the individual disciplines that contribute to educational research and practice—psychology, sociology, economics, and anthropology, among others—have different conceptualizations of innovation (Baregheh, Rowley, & Sambrook, 2009). For example, a sociologist might describe innovation as "the process of introducing new elements into a culture through either discovery or imitation" (Schaefer, 2012, 57). Psychologists, in turn, may focus on the external conditions that encourage creativity and innovation, as well as the innate characteristics of an individual (Kumar &

Bharadwaj, 2016). An individual who works in the information technology department of a university might find the following definition from the Organization for Economic Cooperation and Development (2001) more compelling: "new products and processes and significant technological changes of products and processes." Scholars who work in business management may focus on practical matters, stating that innovation is the "invention and implementation of a management practice, process, structure, or technique that is new to the state of the art and is intended to further organizational goals" (Birkinshaw, Hamel, & Mol 2008, 825). Within the nascent field of innovation studies, researchers have often adopted a general definition of innovation ("new combinations of existing knowledge and resources") that leaves considerable space for expansion (Fagerberg, Fosaas, & Sapprasert, 2012). Meanwhile, many individuals have dismissed innovation as hollow jargon, while others have cautioned that overuse of the term has made it ambiguous and/or inconsequential (Ackermann, 2013; Berkun, 2007; Erwin & Kraksuer, 2004; Feldman, 2002; Page, 2014).

Several authors have lamented this lack of consensus concerning a single, unifying definition of innovation (Adams, Bessant, & Phelps, 2006; Cooper, 1998; Zairi, 1994). To reiterate our introduction, we instead argue that this lack of consensus about innovation need not be viewed as a weakness. One of the attractive qualities about innovation as a concept relates to its transferability and reconceptualization across different disciplinary areas, time periods, and cultures. For innovation to have real meaning in higher education, however, it needs to have a well-defined conceptual field that acknowledges strengths, weaknesses, and challenges. Furthermore, a lexicon of interconnected terms should be defined in order for innovation to have meaning. For these reasons, we propose that one way to define a complex concept such as innovation is to first describe what it is not.

Three Things Innovation Is Not

1. Innovation is Not Unbridled Creativity. It Requires Expertise.

As we detail later in this chapter, two of our fundamental assumptions are that (1) innovation and creativity differ in meaningful and tangible ways and (2) both innovation and creativity are more complex than is implied by the multitude of banal slogans employed by corporate entities. For example, one is likely to encounter the following distinction between creativity and innovation on quote boards, mugs, and various internet memes: "Creativity is thinking up new things. Innovation is doing new things."

Keeping in mind this definition, let's consider the following scenario:

A child is assigned by her art teacher to draw and color a picture, using a cat as a model. In turn, the child creates a drawing that is somewhat abstract by modifying the cat's position, changing the color of the cat's fur, and providing a thought bubble above the cat in which it is imagining a saucer of milk. Is such a drawing creative or innovative? Or, could it be neither?

We suggest that the drawing is creative in that it reimagines the cat in a personal manner and offers a unique interpretation. This assessment already invalidates the above definition of creativity, which contends that creativity is merely related to the act of "thinking." Instead, the child produced a tangible, creative artifact.

Is the drawing innovative? Probably not. One can easily imagine that other people have produced similar drawings (which means it is lacking in *novelty*), and it is unlikely that the child's drawing will deeply influence the future work of a broad spectrum of artists (which means it is lacking in *diffusion* and *impact*).

We will go into more detail about the importance of novelty, diffusion, and impact to the concept of innovation. For now, however, it is simply important to emphasize that trite distinctions between creativity and innovation can stand in the path of deeper understanding. Without additional rigor, the concepts of innovation and creativity could even become ambiguous to the point of insignificance.

As a starting point, it is essential to note that creativity and innovation are grounded in a certain level of knowledge and expertise that is embedded in societal norms and expectations. In order for the child in our example to draw and color a cat with a thought bubble, the child needs to have several essential pieces of knowledge: an understanding of what a cat is and what a cat typically looks like; a sense for whether or not the cat is capable of independent thought; and what the cat might actually think about. The level of expertise is inconsequential because we are not making a judgment about how creative the child's drawing ultimately is. What is significant to point out is that creativity is not "unbridled." Even the most avant-garde artists, musicians, or playwrights rely on technique that is usually developed over many years, a cultural base of understanding embedded in existing artistic practice, the artistic legacies of previous individuals, and an encyclopedic knowledge of acceptable genres. From this base of understanding, a creative artist can build from prior work and/or thwart the culturally grounded aesthetic expectations that they know an audience carries into a performance. Scientists may have a more incremental process when carrying out experiments in a laboratory environment, but their creativity is similarly sparked by years of practice, their specialized acumen, and an inherited sense of what might constitute meaningful development in their chosen field.

2. Innovation is not merely "something new." It is a process facilitated by institutional culture.

One common mistake made by many individuals, as well as companies, is the presumption that an innovation requires only development and production. Once it is completed and readily available, the belief holds, an effective innovation will be immediately recognized and utilized by its target audience.

The reality of most innovations is messier. In our own research on innovation, we have learned that the adoption of an innovation may not occur if the innovation is prohibitively expensive, requires a steep learning curve for operation, or needs further refinement. Even if an innovation seems less expensive, the institutional adoption and implementation of an innovation needs to be motivated by more than a desire for greater efficiency. If an institution's human and digital resources are not capable of supporting a technological innovation, for example, the implementation process will not only be ill-fated, it will be an expensive proposition as well. If a given technological innovation is not intuitive or effective for its intended audience, the supposed gains achieved by greater efficiency will be completely rendered moot (e.g., see Lanford, 2021; Lanford et al., 2019; Lanford, 2016; Lanford & Tierney, 2015).

One might reasonably assume that technology adoption and implementation in the higher education space should be comparable to that of any other organization. And in some ways, it is. Similar to corporations and other organizational entities, colleges and universities generally make decisions about the adoption of specific technological platforms and tools at the institutional level (or even at a more localized departmental level). In this way, higher education is distinct from secondary education, where many of the decisions concerning the institutional adoption of technology may be mandated by district or state policy. Colleges and universities are also like many other organizations in that they are guided by mission statements, have unique institutional environments, and develop processes of socialization whereby individuals learn about the culture of their institution. In turn, each of these elements of institutional culture provides direction, sheds light on the institution's history, and gives shape to contemporary attitudes within the organization.

However, three elements of institutional culture arguably make higher education quite different from organizations in the business world. In fact, higher education has been described as a field of "loosely coupled institutions" with decentralized departments and programs that are resistant to external mandates for change (Weick, 1976; Stensaker, 2015). Whether this depiction is accurate or not, it has implications for three aspects of institutional culture that affect the adoption and implementation of technology: leadership, strategy, and information.

Leadership

Any higher education institution is likely to have a veritable garden of leaders beyond the university president or the provost. Due to their academic experiences and disciplinary expertise, deans and division chairs may enjoy greater legitimacy as leaders within their specific schools and divisions. Moreover, colleges and universities generally have a substantial number of "informal" leaders who are well known and widely respected; their support is necessary for the success of many new initiatives.

Strategy

Strategy can also be complicated within a higher education institution due to widespread expectations of academic freedom and shared governance (Rhoades, 2005). Faculty expect an inclusive decision-making process that solicits the opinions and ideas of individuals who have a stake in a given project's outcomes. Their knowledge and feedback is especially important if they have expertise relevant to a project's goals, even if their understanding of technology is minimal. In instances where these values and expectations are not respected, the strategies of leadership may be undermined, bonds of trust will be damaged, and institutional support for future initiatives is likely to be weakened (Stensaker & Vabo, 2013).

Information

The topic of information is related to leadership and strategy. Unless information is conveyed in a comprehensive and meaningful way to all meaningful stakeholders within a college or university, support for leadership initiatives and institutional strategies is unlikely to be garnered among the faculty and staff of different departments. Increasingly, leaders in higher education have embraced the rhetoric of change and disruption to push innovation, lest a peer institution becomes an early adopter of a new innovation that offers a strategic advantage. Quick decisions may not always be the correct decisions, however. In complex organizations like colleges and universities, feedback from multiple constituencies is vital for the adoption and understanding of an innovation. Communication should not solely exist for the dissemination and implementation of institutional strategies; it should be the cornerstone of a two-way dialogue about what an institution needs and the individuals best positioned to effectively utilize innovations that can meet institutional challenges.

3. INNOVATION IS NOT A SYNONYM FOR TECHNOLOGY OR DISRUPTION.

The mere adoption of technology is not innovative. New technologies have been adopted and executed by individuals working in higher education institutions throughout the twentieth and into the 21st century. Some of those initiatives were even led by faculty, who are too often portrayed by proponents of innovation as "sluggards" and "stragglers" preventing change agents from moving higher education into the 21st century. Moreover, online programs have been offered by a variety of colleges and universities for the past 2 decades, with varying degrees of success. Regardless of the platform, it is peculiar that the creation of an online education degree has almost invariably been accompanied by grand pronouncements that cataclysmic change is on the horizon for higher education—and that colleges and universities that fail to disrupt their normal modes of operation will fall behind and die. Take, for instance, the following quote by Clayton Christensen, the architect of disruptive innovation theory, in 2013:

> I think higher education is just on the edge of the crevasse. Generally, universities are doing very well financially, so they don't feel from the data that their world is going to collapse. I think even five years from now these enterprises are going to be in real trouble (Howe, 2013).

Such pronouncements have obviously not aged well. One instructive example is the case of the University of Florida's venture into fully online degrees, otherwise known as "UF Online." In September 2013, Florida's then Governor Rick Scott authorized the creation of UF Online, allocating $35 million over 5 years to get the program up and running.[6] Additionally, the *Gainesville Sun* discovered (after a dogged public records search that initially—and suspiciously—involved heavily redacted documents) that the University of Florida committed to an 11-year contract with Pearson Embanet worth $186 million.[7] Such a large investment for an unproven platform was quite remarkable (and questionable) for a state that had cut its higher education budget by 30% since 2007.[8] By 2019, the program was supposed to be financially self-sufficient, with the stipulation that Pearson would be paid through a share of tuition revenue rather than by the Florida legislature. Obviously, the University of Florida had every incentive in the world to ensure that its outsized investment in online education would be a success.

Florida's online venture, however, immediately got off to a rough start. The executive director of the program resigned after 2 months on the job. Important questions about shared governance were immediately raised, as faculty involvement in the creation of course content was negligible. From the perspective of administrators, though, the most worrying fact was that the total number of students who enrolled in the program during the first year was approximately 23% below the expectations presented by the business model.

As a result, university officials formulated a new "Pathways to Campus Enrollment" (PaCE) program. Since not enough students were willingly enrolling in UF Online, prospective candidates were simply drafted. As a result, over 3,000 students who applied to the University of Florida for their undergraduate education received welcome news of their acceptance—with a single caveat: they had to take their entire first year of classes online.[9] Naturally, this peculiar decision led to considerable confusion and skepticism. One student stated, "I saw PaCE program, I thought it was some kind of a BS thing . . . I've never heard of it."

The wariness of both students and parents of a program like PaCE was understandable. Questions about the academic rigor of online coursework, as well as their notoriously low completion rates, are likely to persist. However, one other issue worked against UF Online, especially for administrators and policymakers who believed they could simply push students into online coursework by fiat. Quite simply, not enough attention was paid to the individuals who would be adopting the innovation. For example, the same student also made the following remark: "I feel like if I was just taking online classes, it wouldn't be a real college experience."

In a different article, a prospective UF Online student similarly expressed her concerns about the opportunity for networking in an online environment: "As a freshman, I feel like that's the year where you make the most connections and meet everyone. So online I don't feel like you would really have that experience or connection."

Therefore, three issues relevant to the discussion of innovation and technology are apparent through the UF Online example. First, the University of Florida, like similar research universities that have considered moving degree programs online, was the victim of its own marketing success. For years, universities like Florida have sold the "idea" of the college experience. Students from all over Florida want to enjoy the 37,000–square foot student fitness center.[10] They want to meet other college students from around the state. They want to attend concerts and other university-sponsored events that they normally would not get to see in their hometowns. They want to be in Gainesville to experience the atmosphere of a home football game. In essence, they want to build lasting memories in Gainesville—one of many legendary "university towns" across the country that have built a reputation as hubs for academic, artistic, and athletic culture. If it seems far-fetched that universities have successfully sold the notion of the "college life," ask undergraduate students from other countries why they chose to attend an American university. Or, talk with students who express frustration with their "lost year" of college due to the Covid-19 pandemic and found the experience of watching video lessons, navigating learning platforms, and trying to maintain relationships in a virtual space alienating (MacGillis, 2021). Sure, universities in the United States are among the top-ranked institutions in the world, but they also conjure images of an irreplaceable experience in which students learn as much outside of the classroom as they do inside.

Second, based on the paltry enrollment figures and the negative feedback from parents and students, it appears that few individuals associated with higher education in Florida conducted important preliminary research on the viability of convincing 24,000 students to choose UF Online instead of 4 years on the university campus in Gainesville, Florida. Instead, UF Online, as well as a similar failed venture between the California State University system and Pearson, was the product of a business mentality that privileges quick action over careful deliberation, as described by the *Chronicle of Higher Education*: "There was pressure to get the programs up and running quickly, which increased the need for an outside company to handle administrative tasks while the colleges focused on developing course content." Thus, while some may argue that shared governance is a weakness of higher education that paralyzes innovation, this narrative demonstrates how impetuous decision making can foolishly divert scarce resources from institutional strengths that have taken decades to build.

Third, the students interviewed in the UF Online narrative speak to a valuable aspect of face-to-face coursework that has been highlighted in our own research and is difficult to replicate in online environments: meaningful cross-cultural communication and understanding through conversation. This issue is especially important to the students with whom we have worked in education schools, as it directly relates to their potential careers as teachers. For some students in education, face-to-face coursework is the first time they are compelled to interact with peers who come from different cultural backgrounds and socioeconomic classes. Degrees like education require social intelligence and empathy as much as content knowledge. In particular, a future teacher's ability to sympathize with students from a variety of backgrounds is essential. As states like Florida continue to make sizable investments in online education for both K–12 and university students, more questions need to be asked about what might be lost if students and degree programs are siloed in virtual space. To this point, much of the conversation has revolved around economic factors and pedagogical tools. Nevertheless, the possibility exists that a widespread deployment of online education could displace one of the few physical locations where people from different walks of life meaningfully interact, thereby exacerbating the cultural divide in the United States. In this instance, the deployment of technology would not be innovative. Instead, it could be disruptive in a way that diminishes educational experiences instead of enhancing them.

It is important to note here that there have been successful models for the planning, developing, and implementation of online education throughout the landscape of higher education. Western Governors University (WGU), for example, has been a genuinely innovative institution. A private, nonprofit university founded in 1997 by 19 U.S. governors who each committed $100,000 in seed money, WGU uses an online, competency-based educational model that allows students to accelerate through programs if they can draw upon previous work or educational experiences—or simply devote more time to the completion of their degrees (Trow, 1999). While many would reasonably quibble with the comparatively low graduation rates and separation of faculty into mentors, evaluators, and subject matter experts at Western Governors, the institution has been remarkably successful in keeping tuition costs low, maintaining a high degree of student satisfaction, and ensuring that graduates earn post-graduation salaries comparable to peer institutions (Brown, 2018; Shireman, 2018b). Additionally, both the financial health and prospects for longevity appear to be solid; the total student enrollment at Western Governors more than doubled from 53,853 in 2014 to 110,534 in 2018 and is on a consistent pace to increase by approximately 20% each year (Blumenstyk, 2018).[11]

We strongly believe there is a place for innovative institutions like Western Governors University, and we would love to see similarly pioneering ideas take shape in higher education. From the beginning, however, two important factors made Western Governors University different from many of the current online and for-profit institutions that have come and gone over the past 20 years. First, Western Governors University was primarily motivated by a desire to help students achieve a meaningful degree at minimal cost—not simply hand control over the course content to a third-party operation that would feel compelled to make decisions that were in the best interests of shareholders and executives. New institutions and institutional initiatives often suffer from a lack of perceived legitimacy, especially during periods of financial stress or low student enrollment. Western Governors University's student-centered mission, however, conferred a legitimacy to the institution that allowed it to steadily grow over 2 decades and build an identifiable brand.

Second, Western Governors University remained consistent in its mission and its focus. It is one thing for an institution like WGU to market online, competency-based degree programs. Potential students understand the type of institution they are enrolling in, and they can expect few surprises as they pursue their studies. Over time, WGU has also developed a certain level of trust with employers that makes their degree viable in labor markets. It is another thing entirely, however, for administrators at longstanding institutions to quickly develop an "online branch campus" of existing degree programs. Without the buy-in and curricular development of existing faculty and staff, such an initiative is unlikely to succeed. Without effective, regular communication to stakeholders and the honest acknowledgment of emerging challenges to the new model, skepticism will take root. Employers will notice the lack of institutional consistency, question the rigor of the institution's curriculum, and have little interest in hiring the institution's graduates. In fact, the collective institutional memory of harried decision making without the consultation of experts and practitioners may completely undercut future opportunities to innovate.

Conceptualizing Innovation

Having outlined what innovation is *not*, we now turn to the task of conceptualizing innovation. In this section, we will first draw distinctions between innovation and creativity by utilizing examples from music and literature. Through these examples, we shall illustrate that *creativity* and *innovation* have distinct meanings with wide applicability, even across disciplinary boundaries.

Then, we will turn our attention to two concepts that depict aspects of an innovative process or product: *novelty* and *implementation*. This section grapples with the lexical challenges presented by both of these terms in an attempt to clarify what innovation signifies within the field of higher education. A consideration of implementation, in particular, extends the discussion of innovation from the individual sphere to the organizational level.

A final term often conflated with *innovation* is *entrepreneurship*. Scholars and other observers of higher education have long argued that universities must promote an entrepreneurial culture to survive the demands of a globalized marketplace (Clark, 1998) and to support research that can positively impact society (Thorp & Goldstein, 2010). Entrepreneurial goals are distinct from innovative production, though. As we will detail later in the chapter, a better understanding of the relationship between innovation and entrepreneurship can result in greater clarity about when marketization is appropriate for the research a university undertakes or the degree programs a university deploys. Moreover, during our discussion of the environmental factors that simulate innovation, we will demonstrate that a resolute focus on financial profit does not always foster an innovative climate.

CREATIVITY

According to Amabile (1998), creativity results from three qualities—motivation, expertise, and imaginative thinking—possessed by a single individual. Without motivation, a creative thinker is unlikely to have the persistence required to solve a problem requiring knowledge and a willingness to challenge accepted wisdom. A lack of expertise incapacitates motivation and imaginative thinking. Likewise, many individuals have motivation and expertise but lack the imagination to reconceptualize how a new process or product might be adapted to fit a different audience, or even thoroughly reenvisioned to enter a new marketspace.

Creativity is often associated with individual artistic endeavor, especially in dramatic portrayals of tortured artists working in solitude. To be fair, studies indicate that creative people are often independent-minded and willing to take risks (Simonton, 2003). Like many stereotypes, however, the image of the "starving artist" endowed with transcendent, perhaps even prophetic, creative powers that require distance from society is more mythology than fact. Researchers have discovered that positive affective states (Amabile et al., 2005; Fong, 2006), a focus on potential gains (Friedman & Forster, 2001; Lam & Chiu, 2002), and a concentration on distant outcomes (Okhuysen, Galinsky, & Uptigrove, 2003; Forster, Friedman, & Liberman, 2004) each enhance creativity in individuals. In other words, people working within an organization need to feel excited about the work they undertake and believe their work has meaning, even if diffusion and impact are many years down the road. When job satisfaction is high, the creative abilities of individuals are maximized. Since creativity depends on the development of expertise within a given field, and the ability of an individual to both thoroughly understand and build on the work of others, it also may be enhanced through social interaction. Artists and inventors may require occasional solitude to concentrate on cognitive tasks that are especially taxing; nevertheless, creative individuals need to exchange ideas and receive feedback from similarly accomplished peers so they can consider different perspectives, understand the limitations of their own work, and transcend existing boundaries. For years, the fine and performing arts programs within colleges and universities have stimulated creative work through seminars, exhibitions, and juries that socialize artists in precisely this manner (Amabile et al., 1996).

Creativity is also not something that can be simply turned on and off like a water faucet. From an early age, students need to be encouraged to take risks (even if they make mistakes), explore unfamiliar subjects, and be exposed to different cultures. Otherwise, the capacity to think creatively may never be developed as fully as it might. Unfortunately, such an environment is anathema to the current trends of standardized testing, narrowly focused degree programs, and specialization that pervade much contemporary thought regarding education. Later in this chapter we will address how intrinsic motivation also has a fundamental role in stimulating an individual's creative abilities. Once again, though, school and work environments seemingly do little to support intrinsic motivation, instead focusing a great deal of energy on how to assess skill acquisition, develop standards for productivity, and offer financial rewards for the achievement of specific goals.

THE RELATIONSHIP BETWEEN CREATIVITY AND INNOVATION

What distinguishes creativity from innovation? Before considering the relationship between creativity and innovation in higher education, it might be helpful to first compare two well-known composers of Western classical music, Johann Sebastian Bach and Hector Berlioz, who had the motivation, expertise, and imaginative thinking to accomplish feats that evinced significant creative ability. Anyone who has studied *The Musical Offering* or *Goldberg Variations* would attest that Bach was an exceptionally creative composer, endowed with a tremendous capacity for reworking and enlivening musical material that could otherwise sound rather mundane. Despite Bach's prodigious creative gifts as a performer and composer, however, he has not always been viewed as an innovator by musical scholars. While his contemporaries in the early 1700s were experimenting with new musical styles, Bach busily perfected an older contrapuntal style rooted in musical theories and pedagogies from the previous century. Although subsequent composers such as Mozart and Chopin would later diligently study Bach's musical works because of his impeccable technique, they internalized and refashioned many of his contrapuntal and voice-leading practices to suit their own idiosyncratic styles.

By contrast, Hector Berlioz is primarily known today through the innovations he daringly incorporated in his 1830 orchestral masterpiece, the *Symphonie Fantastique*. Written for ninety instrumentalists (the largest number of musicians for its time), the five movement orchestral work challenged numerous musical conventions relating to harmony, rhythm, orchestration, and form, helping to usher in a new age of overtly programmatic music that was emulated by composers throughout Europe for the remainder of the 19th century. No musical scholar would claim that Berlioz was necessarily a superior composer to Bach. In contrast to Bach, though, it is fair to say that Berlioz was both creative and innovative.

In more recent times, one could view the music of numerous jazz and popular artists as similarly innovative. In the 1940s and 1950s, Charlie Parker pushed the limits of what people thought a jazz soloist could achieve through impressive feats of technical skill and improvisatory imagination (Woideck, 1998). Duke Ellington, who wrote more than a thousand compositions in the 20th century with arranger Billy Strayhorn, created an inimitable "big band" that received popular and critical acclaim for its virtuosity, as much as its entertainment value. Ellington's and Strayhorn's stunningly innovative written arrangements have influenced generations of film composers, orchestral musicians, jazz musicians, and music producers (Tucker, 1991; van de Leur, 2002). Berry Gordy was an innovator and an entrepreneur who not only developed the musical talents of numerous influential artists, such as the Supremes, the Commodores, Stevie Wonder, and Marvin Gaye, but also cultivated a unique "Motown" brand that exemplified sophistication and precision. The Motown training of musicians, while intense and damaging for some individuals, has been innovative in that many contemporary genres, such as K-Pop from South Korea, model Motown's fusion of intricate choreography, fashionable presentation, and musical virtuosity.

Similar arguments could be made about creative and innovative figures in other artistic fields, such as literature. With his two-volume work *Don Quixote*, Miguel Cervantes is often credited with writing the first modern European novel. Innovative ideas abound in *Don Quixote*, including a metafictional opening that asserts Don Quixote was a real human being whose chivalrous adventures were chronicled by a Moorish author named Cide Hamete Benengeli and translated from the Arabic language. Characters within the novel, such as Dorotea and Cardenio, tell stories that may or may not be reliable, depending on the reader's interpretation. Additionally, in the second volume of *Don Quixote*, Cervantes includes a major character from a rival author's unauthorized sequel (written under the apparent pseudonym Alonso Fernández de Avellaneda) and has him disavow the "illegitimate" Don Quixote. In short, Cervantes inspired generations of later authors who wished to create alternative histories, compel their readers to grapple with characters' trustworthiness, and blur the lines between reality and fiction (Hathaway, 1995).

William Faulkner, recipient of the Nobel Prize for Literature in 1950, received tremendous critical acclaim for his idiosyncratic depictions of life in rural Mississippi. In works such as *The Sound and the Fury* and *As I Lay Dying*, he employed the narrative techniques of stream of consciousness and shifting first-person narration in an attempt to capture the psychological states of his characters. Other prominent 20th-century authors and filmmakers were deeply influenced by Faulkner, utilizing some of the same narrative techniques to advance their stories. From the perspective of American literature scholarship, then, Faulkner is widely considered to be an innovative author, and his novels are regularly assigned in both high school and college literature classes. Yet many of his most experimental novels never achieved commercial success during his lifetime.

By contrast, Agatha Christie is the best-selling novelist in history, eclipsed in overall sales only by Shakespeare and the Christian Bible. Her novels, short stories, and plays—each exhibiting a masterful control over characterization and narrative direction—are certainly no less creative than Faulkner's. Nevertheless, Christie never experimented with the sorts of literary devices that would be considered "novel" by literary scholars, and many might argue that her detective novels were not necessarily groundbreaking but rather pinnacle achievements within a specific genre (i.e., the detective novel). Thus, from the perspective of literary scholarship, novels like *Murder on the Orient Express* and *Death on the Nile* are seen as more creative than innovative. They are rarely assigned in college literature classes, although Christie achieved tremendous popular and commercial success during her lifetime.

1. NOVELTY

Drawing upon the above examples, *novelty* is the first of two characteristics that differentiate innovation from creativity. Although anthropologists and sociologists developed theories and definitions for innovation in the early 20th century (Godin, 2014), Joseph Schumpeter (2005) most famously addressed this defining characteristic of innovation in his 1932 article, "Development." As mentioned in Chapter 3, Schumpeter's understanding of novelty asserts that both time and the luxury of hindsight can distinguish between a novel product or process and a truly innovative one (Carlile & Lakhani, 2011). As evidenced by the fiery rhetoric with which he occasionally conveyed his ideas, Schumpeter believed that institutions needed to focus on innovation for competitive survival (Dodgson & Gann, 2010). Over the course of the 20th century, Schumpeter's argument has been expanded to encompass the notion that modern societies are dependent upon the conception and implementation of innovative ideas and knowledge to preserve their relative prosperity (Robin & Schubert, 2013). In business and management literature, a hypercompetitive marketplace is therefore a replication of this globalized, inimical environment (D'Aveni, 1994), and it mandates that organizations engage in continuous innovation to maintain their competitiveness and generate new advantages (Dess & Picken, 2000; Tushman & O'Reilly, 1996).

We agree with Schumpeter's assessment, adding only the qualification that novelty is also dependent upon the view from the *field* in which novelty is being assessed. A group of literary scholars who value experimentation in the use of language and psychological states are predisposed to view Faulkner as an innovative author and Christie as a creative one. However, a group of mystery novel aficionados might have a different perspective, asserting that the bold plot devices and nihilistic themes in *And Then There Were None* (in which every major character dies) and *Murder on the Orient Express* (in which nearly every major character is involved in a single murder) have influenced subsequent literary works, theater productions, and screenplays. Thus, they might view Christie as the more innovative of the two authors.

Similar claims could be made in virtually any other artistic genre or field of endeavor, as long as they are grounded in (1) an understanding of what has been accomplished in the past and (2) a recognition of what is novel and influential about an innovation in the present.

2. Implementation

In addition to *novelty*, a second valuable concept that distinguishes innovation from creativity is *implementation*. Each of the above examples concerning musicians and literary figures represent individuals who implemented ideas within a specific artistic genre and were subsequently judged by a critical audience. That audience, over time, assessed the work as creative and/or innovative based on the aesthetics of the prevailing culture combined with historical perspective.

If an artistic idea is not implemented in some way, it still might be recognized as creative. The histories of music, literature, and film are full of intriguing works—such as the vast collection of unreleased musical works by Prince that was stored in a vault throughout his life; Claude Debussy's operatic sketches to *Rodrigue et Chimène* and *The Fall of the House of Usher*; and Jane Austen's novel *Sanditon*—that evince tremendous creativity. Those works could have also been innovative, but they were not influential due to their unfinished state and/or lack of circulation. Another such example is Orson Welles's unfinished film, *The Other Side of the Wind.* Shot over 6 years during the 1970s, *The Other Side of the Wind* anticipated the mockumentary style that would later be popularized by "innovative" films such as *This Is Spinal Tap* and widely popular television sitcoms such as *The Office* and *Modern Family.*

At times, innovations are associated with individuals who produce the most compelling implementation. For example, the musical technique of 12-tone composition was first employed in the 20th century by Josef Hauer, a German composer relatively unknown to contemporary audiences. Later, a group of composers identified as the "Second Viennese School" (perhaps best exemplified by Arnold Schoenberg, Alban Berg, and Anton Webern) produced a series of aesthetically persuasive compositions based on their idiosyncratic deployments of 12-tone technique. Hence, they—instead of Hauer—have become associated with the development and subsequent impact of 12-tone composition as an innovative musical practice.

Hence, implementation is particularly applicable to an organizational understanding of innovation. Without an implementation stage, an organization cannot give a creative idea the opportunity to impact the industry in which it might operate or be subject to evaluation. Whereas *novelty* is subject to the assessment of external forces (Wang & Ahmed, 2004), the process of *implementation* requires internal evaluation by an organization (Crossan & Apaydin, 2010). Typically, an innovative organization is also creative. However, an organization that lacks the capacity for creativity may be able to recognize an innovative product or process and implement another organization's invention. In 1981, for example, Microsoft purchased the DOS operating system from Seattle Computer Products. After making a few modifications, Microsoft then convinced IBM to use DOS on their new line of 16-bit personal computers. Since Microsoft retained the rights to sell DOS to other software companies interested in writing software for the new IBM PCs, it not only became known as a company that specialized in software innovation but also rapidly achieved market dominance by the mid-1980s.

Schumpeter (1939) also recognized the importance of implementation to a comprehensive theory of innovation, arguing that its impetus was traceable to economic impulses. McLean (2005), likely influenced by the work of Schumpeter, claims that a creative organization also needs to be an innovative one because "many brilliant ideas never see the light of day. To bring an idea from concept to market, it must be recognized for its potential" (227). Both authors implicitly make a distinction between an *invention*—a creation that results from intellectual creativity (Godin, 2008; Schumpeter, 1939)—and an *innovation*—a creation that is subject to some type of implementation process initiated by an organization for economic gain.

Unfortunately, the most compelling implementation of an innovative practice does not necessarily become the most famous or financially lucrative. In U.S. musical history, there are numerous examples of Black artists who developed key musical features and stylistic traits associated with blues, jazz, and rock genres, only to watch as white artists received credit and professional rewards for their innovations. Big Joe Turner's version of "Shake, Rattle, and Roll" is today acclaimed as a milestone performance in the history of rhythm and blues, but it was the "white version" performed by Bill Haley, a country music performer previously famous for cowboy yodeling, that sold one million copies in the 1950s. Thus, it is critical to remember that the *reception* of innovations cannot be separated from the biases embedded in society; an innovation may receive belated attention for reasons that have little to do with its potential impact, its creativity, or its utility.

Further, innovations developed in one country may receive greater attention through increased circulation in another country with enhanced resources. One sees this phenomenon most frequently in industries, such as film production, where the United States has had an outsized influence through its distribution networks. To cite one example, U.S. filmmaker George Lucas has readily admitted that Akira Kurosawa's acclaimed 1958 samurai film *The Hidden Fortress* deeply influenced the story structure, character perspective, and union of action and comedy in *Star Wars* (Barber, 2016). While *The Hidden Fortress* was one of the highest-grossing films in Japan, its box office intake paled in comparison to the revenue of the Star Wars franchise, which has totaled more than $10 billion (U.S.). Numerous other innovative films first created outside of the United States, such as *Infernal Affairs* in Hong Kong, have had a relatively limited impact due to distribution. When *Infernal Affairs* was later remade by Martin Scorcese as *The Departed*, Hollywood distribution networks were able to leverage the Warner Brothers media empire—as well as the latter film's all-star cast of Leonardo DiCaprio, Jack Nicholson, and Mark Wahlberg—to garner approximately $300 million (U.S.) at the box office and an Academy Award for Best Picture in 2007.

Creativity and Innovation—on the Organizational Level

Can organizations stimulate the creativity necessary to produce an innovation? Due to bureaucratic policies and procedures, organizations are often portrayed as negative forces that stifle the creative spirit of an individual (Sternberg & Lubart, 1999). Since individuals are inevitably compelled to conform to the expectations of the organization, internal motivation is crippled, the imagination of the individual is stifled, and creativity dies. In fact, one of the cited benefits of universities is that they are loosely coupled systems where a teacher or researcher may work without oppressive regulations and constant supervision (Weick, 1976).

Others view the relationship between creativity and organizations differently, however. Woodman, Sawyer, and Griffin (1993) define organizational creativity as "the creation of a valuable, useful new product, service, idea, procedure or process by individuals working together in a complex social system" (293). This definition depicts creativity as the development of something novel by a group rather than as the product of an individual working in isolation. Indeed, creativity may be enhanced through social interaction, and talent may be developed through socialization (Amabile et al., 1996).

Due to the decentralized environments of most postsecondary institutions, the relationship between creativity and innovation is different for higher education than it is for a business. When a college creates an environment conducive to experimentation in the classroom or an office, creativity is focused on an event (teaching a class) or an act (composing an essay). Individuals working within higher education may have a multitude of opportunities to implement their creative research, art, or pedagogy. Researchers who work in scientific fields like biotechnology and neuroscience may elicit significant interest from private companies. An English professor may publish a collection of poems or even start a publishing company. A specialist in education technology may release online pedagogical tools that provide useful training to a broad audience. However, the creativity of this diverse group of individuals generally stays within the boundaries of a campus. While Florida and colleagues (2006) acknowledge that a university should have a creative role to play in economic development, they also argue that the creation of talent and the promotion of new ideas and diversity are central activities for a university:

> The role of the university goes far beyond the "engine of innovation" perspective. Universities contribute much more than simply pumping out commercial technology or generating startup companies. . . . In short, the university comprises a potential—and in some places, actual—creative hub that sits at the center of regional development. (38)

To summarize, the welfare of most nations (certainly, at least, the United States) depends partly on the ability of its higher education system to be creative. Further, colleges and universities are innovative when (a) an individual's creativity is stimulated through interaction; (b) novel products and processes can be created; and (c) a creative product or process may be implemented.

Entrepreneurship

To retain their relevance in the 21st century, colleges and universities should be creative and innovative, but must they be entrepreneurial? Many have argued that entrepreneurial activities are a natural outgrowth of the entrenchment of neoliberal philosophies in political discourse about higher education. Shahjahan and Hill (2019) have considered the intersection of neoliberalism and higher education at length:

> Neoliberalism also refers to an ensemble of economic argu-
> ments (i.e., logic) making certain material practices and policies
> intelligible, practicable, and governable. Economic rationality
> becomes the overarching frame for understanding, evaluating,
> and governing social life. According to neoliberal logic, society
> should produce self-enterprising individuals solely interested in
> enhancing their human capital. (para 1)

Hence, under neoliberal logic, higher education institutions are compelled to look to the private sector for financial support, and entrepreneurship becomes a more frequently employed concept (Lightcap, 2014). Like innovation, entrepreneurship is a concept that resists easy definition (Low & MacMillan, 1988; Yang, 2012). In fact, substantial overlap exists between definitions of innovation and entrepreneurialism. Yang (2012), for example, argues that entrepreneurship's "defining trait is the creation of a novel enterprise that the market is willing to adopt. It thus entails the commercialization of an innovation . . . By fusing innovation and implementation, it is a unique process that allows individuals to bring new ideas into being for the benefit of themselves and others" (388). Such a definition makes innovation and entrepreneurship sound synonymous.

Differences do exist between innovation and entrepreneurship, however, even if they are subtle. For our purposes, entrepreneurship is distinguished from innovation by the nature of its goal. Innovation in higher education can encompass a broad variety of product- or process-oriented activities with a diverse set of goals, such as social influence, cultural impact, or financial gain. On the contrary, entrepreneurship has as its primary end the accumulation of wealth through new or existing ideas. As such, an entrepreneur is primarily focused on the marketization of an innovation. Based on our previous discussion, Faulkner would likely not be considered an entrepreneurial author. However, Christie's financial success is certainly entrepreneurial in nature, and Berry Gordy was patently successful from any entrepreneurial perspective. Entrepreneurs do not necessarily have to be innovative, but they do have to focus on business goals, management, and financial imperatives when considering the potential impact of an innovation (in particular) or their product (in general).

Higher Education:
An Entrepreneurial or Innovative Enterprise?

This distinction between innovation and entrepreneurship has far-reaching implications for institutional decision making in higher education. Since at least the 19th century, an entrepreneurial spirit, as well as a willingness to adapt to societal needs, has been necessary for many higher education institutions (Kimball & Johnson, 2012). With regards to higher education, however, the implications of a collective mindset oriented toward entrepreneurship versus a collective mindset focused on innovation are worth considering.

To cite but one example, the Bayh-Dole Act, since its inception in 1980, has allowed research universities in the United States to maintain their intellectual property rights, even if federal funds were utilized during the discovery process of a patentable discovery (Perkins & Tierney, 2014; Shane, 2004). Before the passage of the Bayh-Dole Act, less than 5% of the approximately 28,000 patents held by U.S. federal agencies were commercially licensed (USGAO, 1998). However, the effect of the Bayh-Dole Act on university research priorities was immediate and robust (Ezell, 2019). In 1980, only 390 patents were awarded to universities. By 2009, however, 3,088 patents were awarded, and that total more than doubled by 2015, when 6,680 patents were granted to universities throughout the United States. In addition, American universities created more than 2,200 companies to monetize their inventions during the first 2 decades of Bayh-Dole (Rabitschek & Latker, 2005). Advocates of the Bayh-Dole Act argue that it has increased the revenue streams at universities capable of producing patentable research and generated a net positive effect on the U.S. economy (Coupe, 2003; Slaughter & Leslie, 1997; Slaughter & Rhoades, 2004). These perceived benefits have caused other nations to consider similar laws in hopes of encouraging impactful research and stimulating financial revenue streams (Marginson, 2004).

Critics, on the other hand, contend that the Bayh-Dole Act has instigated a fundamental shift in institutional values, as universities are progressively deemphasizing theoretical research in deference to applied research that can be more easily monetized through entrepreneurial ventures (Henderson, Jaffe, & Trajtenberg, 1998; National Science Board, 2008; Powers, 2003). Moreover, the "transactional costs" and exclusive licenses that have resulted from the Bayh-Dole Act prevent researchers from freely sharing discoveries with colleagues (who could similarly advance knowledge) and the general public (who, at least in part, provided financing for the research in the first place) (Kanarfogel, 2009). Since U.S. taxpayers deliver more than $100 billion each year in direct research funding, many are uncomfortable with the notion that consumers pay a second time to use a patented product that was originally developed by a university or other federally funded lab (Hemel & Ouellette, 2017). For these reasons, the entrepreneurial motives that undergird the Bayh-Dole Act have received justifiable scrutiny from many scholars (Kenney & Patton, 2009; Kezar, 2004) but less attention from other stakeholders.

Entrepreneurial goals do not always conflict with a university's mission to serve the public. Insofar as the mission of a university offers meaning, direction, and purpose to institutional actors (Tierney, 2008), though, entrepreneurial motives need to be weighed against other salient goals of a university, such as public welfare and social justice. Through such critical examination, innovative research that can provide broad benefits to society does not become solely directed by financial concerns.

In Summary

Both *creativity* and *entrepreneurship* overlap with *innovation* in specific ways. As can be graphically seen in Figure 5.1, *creativity* refers to inventiveness grounded in field-specific knowledge and expedited by motivation.

While creativity is a necessary condition for innovative thinking, not all creative individuals or organizations have been innovative. *Innovation*, depicted in Figure 5.2, pertains to the implementation of a creative product or process and its perceived novelty once it has been evaluated by a critical audience.

Figure 5.1. Flowchart of Creativity.

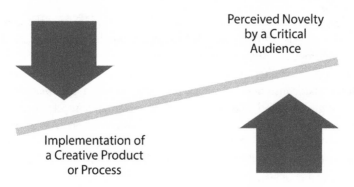

Figure 5.2. Depiction of the Innovation Process.

Entrepreneurial strategies rely on innovation, but innovative thinking is not always motivated, or even induced, by entrepreneurial objectives. For this reason, our focus for the remainder of this book is on understanding innovation, rather than entrepreneurship, in the higher education environment.

Chapter 6

Stimulating Mindful Innovation

Is There a Formula?

With creativity, innovation, and entrepreneurship defined, we now turn to a conceptualization of mindful innovation in higher education. This chapter focuses on the four factors that stimulate innovative activity within organizations: diversity, autonomy, intrinsic motivation, and constructive critique. The next chapter details the dimensions that can help an institution plan, develop, and implement an innovation in mindful manner.

In recent years, design thinking has taken hold as a formula for stimulating innovation in organizations. It began as the primary "methodology for producing reliably innovative results in any field" within the Hasso Plattner Institute of Design (also known as the "d.school") at Stanford University. Since the inauguration of the Stanford d.school in 2005, however, design thinking has been the center of controversy over how unique the methodology is—and whether or not a specific methodology can inculcate people into developing innovations that can create meaningful change. The debates are encapsulated by a paragraph in a 2017 feature on design thinking in the *Chronicle of Higher Education*:

> Some see [design thinking] as a way to better engage a new generation of students. Some see it as a tool to bring fresh thinking to colleges bound by tradition and inertia but operating in an increasingly volatile landscape. The more skeptical see it as yet another corporate-culture fad infiltrating academe and

taking up time and energy that could be spent on the mission. (Gardner, 2017)

The five-stage process of design thinking is as follows: empathizing, defining, ideating, prototyping, and testing. The empathetic stage, also called "ethnography" by design thinking specialists, encourages designers to learn about the needs of individuals, in particular how and why they do things and what they find meaningful. Once information is gained from the empathetic stage, a problem (or opportunity) can be defined and ideas generated. If necessary, design thinking also encourages a redefinition of the problem as new information is gathered and innovative solutions are proposed.

We find much to commend in design thinking, as it emphasizes the importance of considering the target audience while developing a new product or process.[1] It also encourages empathetic qualitative inquiry into the lives of users, diverse perspectives within the design team, and the importance of feedback loops in testing and refining possible innovations. However, design thinking is also problematic in at least three ways. First, it shortchanges the importance of prolonged engagement, the need for reflexivity, and the role of power dynamics in ethnographic inquiry. As any qualitative researcher will know firsthand, a deep understanding of a given phenomenon or group of individuals takes an extended period of time—months, if not years. During that time, researchers may only gradually become aware of their biases, and they are likely to recognize the manifold ways in which participants could be incentivized to tell them what they want to hear. We believe a mindful approach to innovation would engage with ethnographic inquiry on a deeper level, encouraging the people who might be impacted by an innovation to offer their perspectives throughout the innovation's development and implementation. It would also encourage the people working with an innovation to critically reflect on their decisions as the innovative process unfolds, particularly with regards to their original motives and the institution's overarching mission statement.

Second, as we have already argued, the role of expertise in creativity and innovation is essential. One issue many have had with design thinking is with the presumption that anyone can engage in the process and come up with innovative products. While this is certainly possible, it could also result in tragic wastes of time and energy. A mindful innovation approach would view individual expertise from a variety of fields relevant to the creative product or process as vital to the innovation process. Communication across disciplinary boundaries and entrenched institutional hierarchies would also be essential. Moreover, research into other proposed and implemented solutions would be valued, in addition to wisdom gained from others' mistakes.

Third, the evidence validating design thinking as a viable process that promotes sustained innovative activity is scant. If anything, the type of inquiry encouraged by design thinking generally results in simplistic, yet potentially financially lucrative, innovations that are ideal for promotion by marketing departments and capitalization by public/private entities. Mariana Mazzucato (2013) has pointed out, for example, that the design of the iPhone was created at Apple, but the technologies that enabled the iPhone to capture the public's attention—from its global positioning system (GPS) to its capacitive touch-screen display—were largely developed through federally funded research. Perhaps the capacity of design thinking to generate commercial products explains its popularity in the business world—but can a design-thinking process help alleviate some of society's most complex problems? The jury is still out.

Four Factors That Have a Positive Impact on Mindful Innovation

We believe that the cultivation of mindful innovation is not just about collaboration; it is also sensitive to different working styles. Mindful innovation is also a messier process that requires significant levels of expertise from more than one individual, repeated failure, peer critique and refinement, and input from people outside of the academy who will largely be impacted by a given innovation. Therefore, to outline how mindfully innovative activity might be stimulated in colleges and universities, we propose to highlight four factors consistently shown—in empirical literature from business, innovation studies, management, and psychology—to have a positive impact on innovation.

1. DIVERSITY

Research has repeatedly demonstrated that the innovative potential of an organization is unleashed when individuals from a diverse range of backgrounds, proficiencies, and voices are brought together. Feldman (2002), in fact, contends that "innovation, at a fundamental level, is a social process that bridges individuals from different disciplines with different competencies, distinct vocabularies, and unique motives" (48). To be sure, research

Figure 6.1. Four Factors that Stimulate Mindful Innovation.

on diversity indicates that companies that actively promote diverse hiring practices have substantial financial returns (Hunt, Layton, & Prince, 2014). Companies in the top quartile for gender diversity are 15% more likely to have financial returns above the national median. Similarly, companies in the top quartile for ethnic diversity are 30% more likely to have financial returns above the national median.

We should be careful not to gloss over the abilities, experiences, and strengths that each individual possesses. A more comprehensive view should also include acquired competencies, such as knowledge of the humanities and significant, prolonged experience with foreign cultures, in order to fully conceptualize how diversity supports innovation. In fact, studies show that multicultural experiences are positively correlated with desirable creative abilities, such as insight learning, remote association, and idea generation (e.g., Leung et al., 2008).

Other examples of acquired competencies include the ability to speak multiple languages, and to translate sophisticated concepts from one discipline to another. In recent years, liberal arts education has come under attack for offering courses that are not directly translatable to the marketplace. However, other educational systems (such as those in Hong Kong) recently came to realize that the liberal arts provide students with the ability to develop acquired diversity characteristics that are necessary for a contemporary knowledge economy. Therefore, they initiated comprehensive educational reforms so that students might develop cross-cultural fluency, an interdisciplinary mindset, and critical-thinking skills that can stimulate greater creativity and innovation (Lanford, 2016).[2]

On an organizational level, research by Hewett, Marshall, and Sherbin (2013) has established that companies with high levels of diversity among leadership and staff are more innovative and more likely to capture new markets. The reasons are manifold: In such environments, leaders more frequently delegate authority, encourage feedback, and allow for multiple perspectives to be heard. Employees, in turn, feel comfortable proposing new concepts, and information about clients and processes is quickly disseminated throughout the organization. For these reasons, such companies are 45% more likely than nondiverse companies to grow market share within a given market within a year. By drawing upon the acquired knowledge and experience that their employees possess, diverse companies are also 70% more likely than nondiverse companies to capture a new market. In short, an innovative institution is one that remains open to the insights and insider knowledge of individuals who hail from a broad range of multiplex identities and life experiences.

One could extrapolate from this information that a primary reason why many countries with impressive test scores fail to innovate at the same level as the United States has to do with this acquired diversity. The United States' educational system has traditionally emphasized the value of a broad-based education. Unfortunately, much of the rhetoric surrounding education today seems to not only dismiss such an education as antiquated and inefficient but fails to recognize the crucial need to provide students with multiple opportunities to develop a meaningful understanding of different artistic and cultural traditions. If innovative thinking is truly the engine of American economic progress, we cannot simply transmit existing scientific knowledge and expect innovation to mysteriously transpire. We need to recognize the advantages that diversity can offer, and promote the acquisition of diverse talents through a renewed commitment to the liberal and fine arts.

2. Intrinsic Motivation

One critical mistake made by many organizations is to exclusively incentivize performance through extrinsic incentives, such as the promise of financial gain or professional advancement. Extrinsic incentives may have some utility in professions where the accumulation of financial wealth or personal accomplishment is a superseding goal. For many, including several economists (Bénabou & Tirole, 2003; Scotchmer, 2004), these types of extrinsic motivators are necessary tools for rewarding exemplary work and for encouraging desired behaviors. However, they do not generally support the types of meaningful innovation that require sustained cognitive engagement and the tenacity to solve complex problems.

When administrators use extrinsic incentives, individuals generally lose interest once a clearly defined objective is met. As a result, progress on an innovative idea stops at a premature stage. In a summary of research conducted by her team at the Harvard Business School, Amabile (1998) maintains that extrinsic motivators do not "make employees passionate about their jobs. A cash reward can't magically prompt people to find their work interesting if in their hearts they feel it is dull." A meta-analysis on motivation conducted by Deci, Ryan, and Koestner (1990) supports Amabile's premise, asserting that "performance-contingent rewards significantly undermine free-choice intrinsic motivation."

Another problem is that workers will find shortcuts to meet extrinsic, predefined objectives. The field of education has long acknowledged that students motivated via extrinsic factors are more likely to cheat on exams or plagiarize papers than those who are motivated intrinsically (Murdock & Anderman, 2006). A similar relevant trend in higher education concerns the expansion of performance funding, a system that associates state funding for higher education institutions with clear metrics associated with desired outcomes, such as student retention and job placement. The theoretical notion behind performance funding is that institutions, in an effort to receive more funding from their respective state governments, will competitively focus their talent, energies, and resources on improving their statistics in these key metrics. Politicians win if they can point to statistical data that purportedly shows improvement in areas relevant to the assessment of postsecondary institutions. Institutions, in turn, win if they can "perform" better than their peers.

Research that we conducted in Florida, however, revealed that performance funding created conditions untenable for the development of innovative ideas and creative programs.[3] First, the state adopted strict timelines that prevented new ideas from being piloted, examined, and reconceptualized. Second, it placed institutions in competition with each other, so that discoveries which might aid student retention and graduation are "held in-house" and do not contribute to public knowledge. Third, the ways in which performance funding were implemented encouraged resource allocation focused only on the metrics being evaluated, not broader considerations of the institutions' and students' well-being. Fourth, the financial incentives that the state of Florida employed in hopes of stimulating extrinsic motivation have had the unanticipated effect of undermining intrinsic motivation (Lanford, 2021).

As evidenced by the recent scandal involving Wells Fargo, people who work in business environments are no different. When Wells Fargo set quotas widely perceived as unreasonable, thousands of employees invested their "creative" energies on opening fraudulent deposit and credit card accounts simply to meet extrinsic goals. If Wells Fargo had found a way to stimulate its employees' intrinsic motivation to work with customers and develop personal relationships, it might have avoided an embarrassing scandal that tarnished the company's reputation and led to the abrupt exit of its chairman and CEO.

In a college or university environment, most creative thinkers do not enter their chosen fields because they hope to make vast sums of money. Instead, they are motivated by a desire to investigate a specific field. They also have an interest in being surrounded by knowledgeable peers who can provide constructive feedback and improve novel ideas. To stimulate an innovative work environment, higher education institutions need to carefully consider the resources that support individual curiosity and intrinsic motivation. Such resources can vary tremendously, depending on the type of institution, the researcher's disciplinary training, the area in which an administrator works, and other factors.

3. AUTONOMY

Colleges and universities need to be particularly careful about institutionalizing deep cultural traits that can thwart creativity and extinguish promising innovations before they have an opportunity to make an impact. Many institutions with proud traditions like to tout "the X University Way," presumably to distinguish themselves from similar institutions. On the surface, such branding strategies are relatively innocuous. However, if these deep cultural traits start to guide every aspect of institutional life, administrators, instructors, and researchers alike may lose their intrinsic motivation to propose and test new ideas.

Innovation can be inhibited by inadvertent disincentives. Stable organizations regularly have "deep cultural traits" that impede change or prevent the adoption of an innovation. At times, these cultural traits can be valuable, particularly if they raise germane skepticism about the implementation of an untested educational fad. However, the institutional culture of a stable organization could also become too "risk-averse," precluding researchers from proposing and testing radical theories, administrators from piloting new management strategies, and teachers from attempting innovative pedagogical tools in their classes. Hasanefendic and colleagues (2017) have shown that change in higher education environments is often attributable to highly skilled individuals who have robust social networks and a strong intrinsic motivation to transform their institutions. And, as previously discussed, intrinsic motivation is a vital factor for the strategic creation and implementation of an innovation. Psychological research consistently shows that intrinsic motivation is deeply intertwined with autonomy (Fisher, 1978; Ryan, 1982); the loss of autonomy begets the loss of intrinsic motivation, and such losses almost invariably cause talented individuals to seek out new working environments.

Excessive evaluation is another institutional process that can negatively affect innovation (Amabile et al., 1996). Some evaluation procedures are, of course, necessary to align program goals with the institution's mission statement, provide data for continued self-assessment, and ensure quality. Nevertheless, onerous evaluations can consume energy, divert precious resources better allocated to other tasks, and discourage individuals from considering a creative (and potentially innovative) idea that could positively impact the university community. Evaluations that penalize individuals for piloting novel concepts are even worse, as people need the autonomy to debate and implement ideas even if a "negative" outcome results. Albert Einstein famously emphasized the importance of failure to his own work, observing, "that fellow Einstein makes things convenient for himself. Each year he retracts what he wrote the year before" (Ohanian, 2008, 253).

The process of experimentation and peer review necessary for scientific progress requires a certain amount of tolerance for error. Karl Popper, a distinguished philosopher of science who specialized in the scientific method at the London School of Economics, eloquently described this milieu, stating that "science is one of the very few human activities—perhaps the only one—in which errors are systematically criticized and fairly often, in time, corrected. This is why we can say that, in science, we often learn from our mistakes, and why we can speak clearly and sensibly about making progress there" (1963, 78). To challenge conventional wisdom, scientists regularly advance unpopular ideas that may be initially flawed, yet undergo refinement over time. Hypotheses are regularly proven false, the methodologies employed to investigate a particular problem are often found inadequate, and changing cultural and societal conditions necessitate the continual reevaluation of longstanding theories. Over time, progress occurs because researchers learn from their mistakes. Through this process, research can lead to important technological advances, such as the mapping of the human genome, thereby positively impacting the overall quality of life for millions of people. If external evaluations focus too narrowly on short-term results without a broader view of the progress that is being achieved, innovation will be stifled.

On the one hand, colleges and universities need evaluative measures that maintain institutional focus and provide actionable information. On the other hand, the professional expertise of individuals working in higher education institutions needs to be respected. No institution can be innovative if it is micromanaged in a way that hinders intrinsic motivation and autonomy.

4. From "Collegiality" to "Constructive Critique"

The successful intersection of diversity, intrinsic motivation, and autonomy in supporting innovation depends on other dimensions, such as time, efficiency, and trust. Each of these dimensions can either positively or negatively impact innovation in higher education, and they will be treated in greater detail in the next chapter. However, an additional concept that has assumed a station of fundamental importance to academic institutions, from community colleges to research universities, is "collegiality." Simply put, collegiality is a cooperative relationship between colleagues founded upon respect. Typically, it entails three elements: (1) disciplinary collaboration for the advancement of knowledge; (2) service through "academic citizenship"; and (3) shared governance through collective decision-making processes (Kligyte & Barrie, 2014; Macfarlane, 2016). Virtually no one relishes abrasive confrontation, particularly when an individual's response seems out of proportion to the importance of the issue under discussion. Nearly every academic has experienced an anxious moment or two during meetings that were extended due to seemingly endless, boisterous debates about relatively minor issues. Moreover, no one delights in the idea of a corporate culture like that at Amazon, where, according to the *New York Times*, a belief system grounded in the idea that "conflict brings about innovation" results in the following outcomes: adversarial relationships between employees, the expectation of availability 24 hours a day for white-collar workers, and admonishment for any employee who fails to prioritize work ahead of a serious illness or family emergency.[4]

The notion of collegiality can be important in ensuring that power relations between administration and faculty, tenured faculty and nontenured faculty, or faculty and students are somewhat mitigated, and that dialogue between parties with unequal power is enabled. For these reasons, collegiality has been thought to contribute to an institutional culture that encourages creativity and innovation in higher education (e.g., Peters, 2019). We agree with the concept of collegiality in theory. One could argue that considerate, measured dialogue is vital for diverse viewpoints to be voiced and heard. For her 2018 book entitled *The Fearless Organization*, Amy Edmondson, the Novartis Professor of Leadership and Management at Harvard University, cogently summarized twenty years of research on creative and innovative companies by arguing the following:

> People must be allowed to voice half-finished thoughts, ask questions from left field, and brainstorm out loud; it creates a culture in which a minor flub or momentary lapse is no big deal, and where actual mistakes are owned and corrected, and where the next left-field idea could be the next big thing.

For people to express themselves and constructively critique their colleagues, we would argue that higher education institutions should promote a collegial environment built on trust. Edmondson (2018) uses the term "psychological safety" to depict similar conditions necessary for creativity and innovation:

> When people have psychological safety at work, they feel comfortable sharing concerns and mistakes without fear of embarrassment or retribution. They are confident that they can speak up and won't be humiliated, ignored, or blamed. They know

they can ask questions when they are unsure about something. They tend to trust and respect their colleagues (xvi).

While acknowledging the potential positive impact of a collegial environment on innovation, we have concerns that accusations levied against faculty members who allegedly lack the capacity for "collegiality" reveal a darker impulse: the desire to stifle dissent and promote a single, uncomplicated vision of higher education.[5] For example, recent research has shown that the rhetoric of "collegiality" inhibits constructive discussions about equity in faculty hiring processes (Liera, 2020). Such an atmosphere is not healthy for any institution of higher education, be it a research university, a comprehensive university, a liberal arts college, or a community college. We thus believe that boisterous debate in the form of "constructive critique" is markedly preferable to total acquiescence.

This issue is especially troubling in the current moment. Fallout from the Covid-19 pandemic is renewing imprudent calls for (1) hasty decision-making processes by small groups of board members and administrators; (2) authoritarian movements to stifle critical inquiry and discourse; and (3) a preference for untested entrepreneurial solutions to complex societal problems over nuanced input from humanistic and scientific experts. In the field of higher education, these developments have resulted in ill-advised decisions to compel in-person coursework; sharp increases in joblessness among racially minoritized groups; overt and implicit threats to students and professors by university administrators and national leaders; and disastrous public-private partnerships that purportedly generate revenue but have decidedly negative impacts on student outcomes, faculty careers, and university culture (Harper, 2020; Redden, 2020; Seltzer, 2020). They have also led to superficial calls for "innovation" by prominent leaders in the higher education sector with no attendant understanding of the conditions that might promote such innovative activity.

One of the first authors to address the topic of innovation and entrepreneurship in higher education was Burton Clark, a professor of education at the University of California at Los Angeles who passed away in 2009 after an illustrious, international scholarly career that included numerous awards from the American Educational Research Association and a Comenius Medal from UNESCO for his contribution to educational development. One of his most influential texts is *Creating Entrepreneurial Universities: Organizational Pathways of Transformation*, a 1998 book that examined five relatively new universities in Europe that had developed a culture of entrepreneurialism presumably worthy of emulation by other ambitious academic institutions. The five elements he found essential for "institutional transformation" were (1) a strengthened steering core; (2) an expanded developmental periphery; (3) a diversified funding base; (4) a stimulated academic heartland; and (5) an integrated entrepreneurial culture. This conceptual framework has been influential in that it has given rise to a sentiment among many observers of higher education that "the strengthened steering core" demands a certain orthodoxy in beliefs about not only the need for change, but also acquiesce concerning the manner and direction of change. Take, for instance, Burton Clark's discussion of "collegiality" at the University of Warwick, one of his five model institutions for "the entrepreneurial university":

> When the University of Warwick can speak proudly of the War-
> wick Way, and faculty there tell of how pleased they were to leave
> their former stodgy universities where nothing got done—and
> morale was very low—to come to a place where problems are
> turned into opportunities and the whole institution has a sense
> of self-directed forward motion, then collegiality favors change,
> not the status quo or status quo ante.

Today, one could make the case that nearly every institution of higher education is entrepreneurial in some manner. As we stated in the previous chapter, with government funding for higher education diminishing in many countries—including the United States, the United Kingdom, and Australia—there is nothing inherently wrong with colleges and universities seeking new revenue streams through entrepreneurial ventures. However, many entrepreneurial perspectives include the misguided philosophical belief (largely adopted from business schools) that the directives of omniscient administrators must be followed, to the letter, for institutional survival during a turbulent period of disruption. Faculty dissent is viewed as the enemy of progress, not as a legitimate concern expressed by people with years, even decades, of valuable, firsthand experience.

The desire for such unquestioning acceptance poses a major problem for the accommodation of diverse perspectives, intrinsic motivation, and autonomy. What about the highly intelligent, deeply committed faculty at Warwick—and other institutions—who hold informed opinions that disagree with institutional directives? If they challenge the "entrepreneurial 'status quo,'" should their voices simply be muted? Must the offending faculty members who do not practice "total buy-in" be sent packing?

Collegiality should not be determined by an individual's willingness to unreservedly embrace administrative edicts. Nor should collegiality be assessed by the degree to which (in Clark's words) "the campus culture becomes integrated around a sense of joint effort" (18). Integration around agreed-upon objectives is a wonderful goal, but it needs to come about through a process of deliberation facilitated by shared governance. Academics are enculturated through graduate training to be critical thinkers, to challenge accepted views, and to engage in constructive critique. Disciplinary progress and innovation cannot occur without skepticism and interrogation. It is highly doubtful that every professor hired at Warwick over the past 30 years or so has been completely happy with Warwick's institutional culture and has had a "passionate attachment to the institution" (18) that superseded their commitments to seeking disciplinary understanding and social justice. A critical mindset is necessary not only to ensure higher education's continued relevance in this critical juncture of human history but also to certify that marginalized voices are heard and the current "K-shaped recovery" is disrupted in favor of a more equitable regeneration of social programs and economic resources.

Collegiality in higher education should not simply involve immediate agreement with a board resolution or an administrative decision. Collegiality should instead depict an environment where dissenting opinions are welcomed and encouraged, even when they do not correspond with the expected status quo. In essence, many current boards of trustees, administrators, and other influential stakeholders are confusing "collegiality" with "conformity," and we believe that is a troubling development for the future of higher education.

Chapter 7

Planning, Developing, and Implementing a Culture of Mindful Innovation

Moving from Efficiency to Empowerment

We believe that a careful understanding of the social, cultural, and economic impacts of innovative change are vital if any higher education institution is to survive the challenges looming in coming decades. For instance, faculty and staff who voice complaints about online education are not necessarily luddites wedded to tradition. They may have important critiques grounded in disciplinary expertise, pedagogical experience, and insider knowledge about their unique student populations. Their feedback can improve the quality of education currently being offered in our colleges and universities much more than any expensive technological fad or overpriced guest speaker.

It is also simply not appropriate to casually wave off legitimate concerns about the adoption of a new technology or potentially innovative program. Those who do run the risk of behaving like Alan Greenspan in 2002, when he extolled the virtues of the "derivatives market" as an "innovation" that could "create economic value." As you may remember from Chapter 2, Greenspan's advocacy of unfettered regulation of the derivatives market was one of the leading contributors to the 2007 financial crisis and indescribable financial and personal pain for millions of people. During the same 2002 speech cited in Chapter 2, Greenspan casually dismissed individuals who were wary of derivatives for having a "deep-seated aversion to the distress that often accompanies the process of creative destruction."

Surely, we in higher education can have a more humane, better informed, and much more mindful response to innovation than what Greenspan exhibited. One way we can do better is by rethinking the way we support innovation, as well as the types of innovations that are supported. In this section of the chapter, we will follow the lead of Janeway (2012) and Christensen (2013), who have each compellingly argued that complex "empowering" innovations—that are frequently difficult to develop, time consuming, and may not be immediately profitable—are necessary for societal progress. Unfortunately, though, much energy is focused on "efficiency" innovations that improve the profit margins of companies and entrepreneurs, yet may have an overall negative effect on the quality of a product or service.

To imagine a mindful approach to the innovation process, we canvassed scholarly literature from psychologists, sociologists, and other scholars interested in organizational productivity. Their work consistently shows that the relationship of three dimensions—time, efficiency, and trust—with innovation is critical for understanding how an innovation may unfold within organizations and society. Each dimension poses challenges for the development of innovations, the conditions that allow for novel or creative thinking, and the sharing of information that inspires an innovative product or process.

1. TIME

Arguably, the most valuable resource is time. As we previously contended, society needs "empowering innovations" that require deep investments of time and resources but can ultimately further economic progress in unexpected

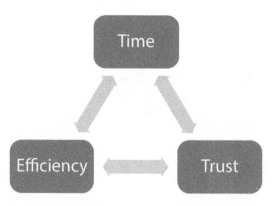

Figure 6.1. Three Dimensions of the Mindful Innovation Process.

ways, thereby improving the overall quality of life for millions of people. One company that developed numerous "empowering innovations" was Xerox PARC. From the 1970s to the 1990s, Xerox PARC was a powerhouse of innovation, developing laser printing technology, graphical interfaces, and many other technologies that powered the personal computing industry (Hiltzik, 1999). As described by Ness (2015), two factors that enabled the company to be so innovative included "funding" and "concentrated brainpower" (37). Most important, however, researchers at Xerox PARC were given a considerable period of time to develop their ideas and bring them to market. This temporal dimension is essential for innovation, as "empowering innovations" may take anywhere from 5 to 10 years (or more) for development, introduction, and diffusion. For this reason, institutions need to carefully interrogate the length of their commitment to funding potentially innovative programs and research. In many cases, long-term funding that gives individuals the time to diagnose problems and correct errors is necessary for substantive innovations that can propel national and regional growth in today's knowledge economy.

The linear process model, developed through a confluence of natural scientists, researchers from business schools, and economists, has been particularly influential on theoretical conceptions of innovation. According to the linear process, basic research initiates the innovation process; this process is followed by a middle stage of applied research and development and ends with a final stage of production and diffusion (Godin, 2006). Critiques of the linear process have been levied throughout the 20th century (Rosenberg, 1994), and numerous alternative models that include multiple feedback loops (Kline & Rosenberg, 1986) and rather complex integrated networks that include external ideas (Galanakis, 2006; Trott, 2005) have been proposed. Nonetheless, the linear process model has proven resilient, partly due to its lasting popularity among policymakers attempting to understand how research and development impacts the economy (Crescenzi & Rodríguez-Pose, 2011).

Therefore, the connection between time and innovation can be considered in one of three ways: (1) the rate of development; (2) the moment in which an innovation is unveiled to the public; and (3) the rate of adoption or acceptance by a given participant base (Dodgson & Gann, 2010). These three stages provide a useful framework for considering the viability of an innovative idea, the resources necessary to realize the development of an innovation, and the likelihood of an innovation's adoption or acceptance by targeted audiences.

Individual disciplines may have different expectations concerning the rate of development for an innovation. For instance, a discipline that deals with continuous technological advancements, such as the digital humanities, may expect new innovative discoveries on a yearly, if not monthly, basis. Conversely, universities may take several years to develop a new drug in partnership with a pharmaceutical company. They may also need to anticipate an extended period of time to ensure safety through multiple drug trials.

Since compressed time can allow innovators to beat competitors to the marketplace, speed during the development stage is typically viewed in a positive light (Vaitheeswaran, 2012). Furthermore, creativity can be stimulated by milestones and deadlines that motivate individuals to complete tasks (Eisenhardt & Tabrizi, 1995), share their work (Takeuchi & Nonaka, 1986), and remain within the confines of a prearranged budget (Drucker, 2014). Nevertheless, people avoid the complex cognitive processing obligatory for innovation if they are constantly working under deadlines (Amabile, Hadley, & Kramer, 2002). This complex cognitive processing often requires patience. As described by Ness (2015), Bell Laboratories was "perhaps the most celebrated dynamo for industrial discovery" because "its parent company, AT&T, did not require fast wins":

> Indeed, they were known for introducing new products and services after a slow and costly process of discovery and development. The mega-corporation could afford to finance basic discovery in physics, mathematics, materials science, and engineering because the Bell system had become colossal. . . . AT&T's progressive leadership invested their proceeds in basic research that built the future of communications and the betterment of humankind. (36)

Both the introduction and the adoption of innovations are subject to a complex array of considerations. When an innovation is brought swiftly to market, companies and individuals alike may be rewarded handsomely for their impetuosity. Likewise, rapid adoption of a promising innovation can lead to competitive institutional advantages within a given field or market. However, employees may be reluctant to undertake the training necessary to effectively utilize an innovation and benefit from its advantages. Some groups may also be disinclined to adapt to innovative products or fully understand their benefits (Rogers, 2003).

2. Efficiency

In certain situations, a focus on efficiency can stimulate creative solutions to demanding problems, especially if resources are limited. Generally, though, efficiency is a disincentive that precludes innovative inquiry. Some even contend that efficiency is the "enemy of innovation" (Janeway, 2012), as it negatively impacts the trial-and-error process necessary for innovation. A reluctance to fund promising research and adequately regulate the tradeoff between efficiency and innovation has triggered significant losses for companies like Motorola, Ericsson, and Samsung (Christensen & Raynor, 2003).

Christensen and van Bever (2014) have astutely argued that far too many companies are currently engaged in "efficiency innovations" that reduce costs on a product or a service. These innovations are attractive because they are often easy to conceptualize and provide a quick return on investment. In 2013, Clayton Christensen also offered a startling rebuke of the "efficiency" model:

> It looks like the economy is emerging from the recession in an exciting way, but we're not creating more jobs or income for the average person. And in all humility, I think I articulated a simple model that explains why. The bad actors are business school professors like me who have been teaching people what I call the Doctrine of New Finance. We've encouraged managers to measure profitability based on a return on net assets, or return on capital employed. That encourages companies to liberate their capital, so they invest in efficiency innovations, which means they can make more money with fewer resources. But what the economy ultimately needs are empowering innovations—like the Model T, the transistor radio. Empowering innovations require long-term investments, which tie up capital for years and years. So companies are using capital to create more capital, and consequently the world is awash in capital but the innovations we need to advance aren't there. (Howe, 2013)

In short, "efficiency innovations" may be held in great esteem by shareholders, but they are not as beneficial to society as "empowering innovations" that make expensive products affordable and create the conditions for economic growth.

3. TRUST

Research concerning the intersection of innovation and higher education usually focuses on institutional structures. Weick (1976), for instance, postulated that educational organizations might be "most usefully viewed as loosely coupled systems" (16). Among many characteristics, these systems are distinguished by their lack of coordination, relative absence of regulations, infrequent inspection of activities, and overall decentralization.

If an educational institution is indeed loosely coupled, then what enables the independence and decentralization necessary for our conceptual framework of innovation? As stated by Molina-Morales, Martínez-Fernández, and Torló (2011), the literature on trust indicates the following:

> Trust helps facilitate cooperation, lowers agency and transaction costs, promotes smooth and efficient market exchanges, and improves firms' ability to adapt to complexity and change. This stream of research holds that firms can find a wealth of benefits from trust, including cost savings and enhanced organizational capacities. (118–119)

Thus, trust can be a crucial animating force that allows talented innovators to enjoy the privilege of autonomy, thereby also enabling intrinsic motivation. In diverse settings, trust can also foster collaboration, allowing for the sharing of information and expertise, rather than siloed knowledge and resources that would occur in a less trusting environment (Ahuja, 2000; Daft & Becker, 1978; Tsai & Ghoshal, 1998). According to Powell, Koput, and Smith-Doerr (1996), innovation may even depend on the relationships that can be forged by individuals from discrete backgrounds.

Although trust exists between two parties writ large, it is, at its most rudimentary level, an interaction between two individuals. This interaction unfolds in a dynamic process and is developed through recurrent interactions between individuals. Over time, greater trust is formed as individuals behave in a manner consistent with predetermined expectations (Seligman, 1997) and greater familiarity is established (Strasser & Voswinkel, 1997). However, greater trust entails greater risk and vulnerability as the potential for digressions from expected behavior exist (Six & Sorge, 2008). Although trust may take considerable time to develop on a meaningful level, it can be invalidated by a single deviation from established norms and/or values (Sitkin & Roth, 1993). This precarious nature of trust, particularly since it involves a combination of emotional and rational behaviors (Bigley & Pearce, 1998), means that individuals differ in their proclivity to trust others (Elangovan & Shapiro, 1998).

On an organizational level, trust can also have an impersonal dimension (Brennan, 1998). If an organization fosters extensive trust, a feeling of relative independence and autonomy may be prevalent among the members of that organization. If trust is weak on the organizational level, however, the members of an organization may feel stifled by extensive control mechanisms (Das & Teng, 2001; Gillespie & Dietz, 2009).

We define trust as "a dynamic process in which two or more parties are involved in a series of interactions that may require a degree of risk or faith on the part of one or both parties" (Tierney, 2006, 57). Consistent with the notion that trust is a dynamic process, we also contend that trust is a social construction, subject to meaning only within specific contexts and situations. A certain degree of uncertainty is vital for both trust and innovation, but the tolerance for that uncertainty is contingent on both cultural and temporal factors.

Trust should not be equated, however, with a lack of supervision or monitoring. Research has also shown that organizations with too much trust may be inefficient, misallocate resources, or lack coordination between different departments (Langfred, 2004; Orton & Weick, 1990). Perhaps even worse, an organization with an abundance of trust will take unnecessary risks based on incomplete data (Molina-Morales et al., 2011).

As mentioned previously, the entrepreneurial desires of the modern university may not always match the intrinsic motivations of researchers and/or administrators to tackle issues involving public welfare or social justice. If the intrinsic motivation of students and faculty is betrayed by the monetization of their work, trust can also erode. Along the same lines, established codes may be necessary to detail and clarify the intellectual property rights of researchers, as well as their ability to participate in open source development that can befit the public good (Välimaa & Hoffman, 2008). Although codes should not tell individuals in a college or university precisely what to study, how to conduct innovative research, or how to establish an innovative policy, they can set the basis for trust and autonomy by outlining broad expectations and letting people with expertise discover new solutions.

If trust is to be engendered by a college or university, the environment should, above all, allow for an open discussion of ideas, even when opinions diverge. Transparency among stakeholders is also crucial. Most effective are intangible constructs that preserve open lines for communication, as well as respect for the roles of researchers and administrators. The confluence of the above factors is vital for an innovative environment (Tierney, 2006).

Summary

Each of the three dimensions—time, efficiency, and trust—discussed in this section require deliberation about an institution's goals, priorities, and culture. While efficiency is generally seen as an "innovation killer," it can also stimulate creative thinking. In general, however, "empowering innovations" that can have the greatest impact on society require considerable time to develop and implement. Since grants typically run for less than 5 years, governments and institutions may want to make lengthier financial commitments, depending on the intended scope and impact of a given project. For such long-term projects, there is a tendency to micromanage the activities of researchers. Hence, trust is of major importance because it diminishes the need for bureaucratic impediments that can increase expenses and stifle creativity. Accordingly, we believe time, efficiency, and trust need to be fostered concurrently within organizations for a culture of mindful innovation.

The Mindful Adoption and Implementation of Foreign Innovations

Thus far, we have talked about four factors that can stimulate mindful innovation and three dimensions of innovation that can help institutions plan for mindful innovation as a process. But what about an institution considering how to mindfully adopt and implement an innovation developed somewhere else? One of the most common errors among educational leaders and practitioners is the assumption that what works in one institutional culture can simply be adopted and implemented, without significant planning and adaptation, in a new institutional culture.

As discussed in previous chapters, innovations can address manifold concerns in higher education and can be tailored for a diverse set of audiences. Some innovations are designed to be wide ranging, such as the recent proliferation of student-advising and monitoring systems that endeavor to improve persistence and graduation rates. Meanwhile, other tools target a niche issue, such as "nudging" applications that remind college-bound students about upcoming deadlines and activities.

Since much of the decision making in higher education occurs at the institutional level, what we propose is for decision makers within an institution to mindfully consider the implications of adoption and implementation of an innovation in three ways: (1) its institutional fit; (2) its potential impact; and (3) its likely longevity. This framework builds from the empirical research outlined above and our own experiences with building support for innovation in our work with a variety of secondary and higher education environments (e.g., Lanford et al., 2019).

Institutional Fit

A new innovation can generate considerable excitement. When the effectiveness of an innovation is backed by evidence of impact within an institution (or group of similar institutions), the euphoria surrounding its arrival can make seemingly intractable problems seem accessible. The problem of replicability in education, however, is worthy of deeper interrogation. As Robert Arnove (2003) has wisely counseled, "the school system of each country reflects the corresponding sociocultural systems within which they are embedded. One cannot simply uproot elements of one society and expect them to flourish in the soil of another society" (7). Higher education is marked by many types of institutions with different mission statements, environments, and socialization processes. What shows promise in a research university may not work, or even be applicable, to the needs of a community college. Private and public institutions often have different sources of revenue, as well as different agencies with whom they are accountable. Moreover, a community college in an urban environment that principally serves as a feeder institution for a local state university may have completely different concerns and issues than a community college in a rural town that serves largely vocational needs.

The heterogeneity of American higher education has historically been viewed as a strength. Thus, a thorough accounting of institutional resources that can complement and sustain an innovation is obligatory if the tool is going to have a fair chance of being accepted. Additionally, the human capital needed to support the innovation should be assessed. There may be times in which the only human resources necessary for support can be found in information technology departments. As Daniel (2015) observes, however, "there is a divide between those who know how to extract data and what data are available, and those who know what data are required and how it would best be used" (916). Hence, at other times, a great deal of faculty and/or staff training may be required so that individuals who might benefit the most from using the innovation have an opportunity to develop a reasonable level of proficiency with it, rather than ignore its existence.

Potential Impact

Once the institutional fit has been determined, the potential impact of the innovation—and for which communities—should be scrutinized. One unfortunate blind spot of technology implementation in higher education, for example, concerns the adoption of digital tools that work reasonably well with robust campus infrastructure but are problematic for students who lack state-of-the-art equipment at home. This problem is especially acute for students who may work full time and enroll in a large number of online classes.

For years, online learning has been heralded as an innovation that could decrease the costs of higher education, especially for students where college options are limited by geography and/or insufficient transportation (Deming, 2015). Neither online learning nor digital tools are a panacea for ensuring that low-income students receive adequate college guidance. Digital access remains a significant barrier to equity. Approximately 57% of families earning less than $25,000 per year have access to a computer at home (Tate & Warschauer, 2017), and a mere 47% of households with yearly incomes under $20,000 have broadband access (Sisneros & Sponsler, 2016). Many rural areas throughout the United States still have difficulties in securing stable, cost-effective internet access (Bjerede, 2018). Even when students have the ability to access relevant and up-to-date materials relating to the college application process, the information may not be readily understood (Brown, Wohn, & Ellison, 2016).

To be useful for low-income and historically marginalized student populations, we propose that online tools should have at least four characteristics. First, they should be inexpensive, if not free, so that students from a broad array of backgrounds can benefit. Second, they should be available on a variety of devices (including computers, tablets, and cell phones) and operating systems (including Apple iOS, Google Android, and Microsoft Windows, among others). Third, they should be accessible to students who may not have access to technology outside of an educational setting. Fourth, they should provide opportunities for networking so that students, faculty, and other stakeholders can share their knowledge and experience, thereby extending the viability of the platform.

Likelihood of Longevity

One worrying trend in higher education concerns the use of innovative programs and practices to displace skilled human labor, particularly in areas like advising that necessitate social and cultural awareness as much as disciplinary and institutional knowledge. Usually, the justification for such changes revolves around issues mentioned in Chapter 2: the continued defunding of higher education and the need for greater institutional efficiency. To this end, some researchers and observers of higher education have called for tools that can usher in a "Netflix for education" era by collecting, analyzing, and personalizing immense streams of institutional data, particularly about students (e.g., Kalamkarian, 2017a, 2017b; Mehta & Harles, 2017).

What we have learned in the past few years, however, is that innovations are usually only one aspect of a multifaceted effort to improve areas of institutional performance, such as student engagement, persistence, and success. For example, a digital platform called "Degree Compass" at Austin Peay State University had much initial success in giving students helpful suggestions about which classes and degree pathways they were most likely to be successful in. From 2010 to 2014, the platform boasted a 90% success rate at predicting whether a student would pass a given class, and the university's 6-year graduation rate improved from 33% to 37.4% (Johnson, 2018). By 2017, however, Austin Peay's graduation and retention rates regressed to pre-2010 levels due to a lack of on-campus residential housing, leadership and advising turnover, and changing student demographics. Even more troubling was the concern that Degree Compass was amplifying biases based on ethnicity, gender, and race and encouraging students to avoid challenging coursework.

Concluding Thoughts

Innovations can address manifold concerns in higher education and can be tailored for a diverse set of audiences. Some innovations are designed to be wide-ranging, such as the recent proliferation of student advising and monitoring systems that endeavor to improve persistence and graduation rates. Meanwhile, other innovations target a niche issue, such as "nudging" applications that remind college-bound students about upcoming deadlines and activities.

Regardless of an innovation's purpose or intent, however, it is still limited by the factors outlined in this institutional framework: the tool's institutional fit, the tool's potential impact, and temporal factors that affect the tool's longevity. Through a systematic consideration of these factors, institutions will be better positioned to assess the innovations continuously being marketed and promoted in today's burgeoning tech space. More importantly, though, they will be able to critically examine how those innovations could both positively and negatively impact the individuals who comprise higher education's increasingly diverse and vibrant campus space.

Chapter 8

Not So Fast! The Shortcomings of Current Rhetoric on Innovation

Graveyards of Innovation?

One of the historically common assumptions about higher education is that it is moribund and resistant to change. Calvin Coolidge reportedly joked, "Changing a college curriculum is like moving a graveyard: you never know how many friends the dead have until you try to move them!" The presumed culprit is the faculty. We are resistant to change. Those who are the defenders of academe frequently respond that colleges and universities are among the world's oldest institutions; resistance to disrupting something that has been around for centuries is not a weakness, but a strength.

We appreciate the criticism and response. In an environment where consensus is valued and individuals have trained their entire professional lives to develop world-class expertise in their respective fields, change will not be easy. Insofar as faculty have diverse opinions and beliefs about the shape of their own work, change will involve seemingly endless dialogues, debate, and compromise. Some believe, for example, in a more open-ended general curriculum to create an informed citizenry, and others will opt for a discrete and finite general curriculum where students study intensively in a single major area. When we combine intellectual beliefs with the practical implications about how such decisions change an individual's work life, the result can be a resistance to change.

A reasoned response can also be that knowledge dissemination in one's research and teaching should not be susceptible to fads and whims. Indeed, in an organization ostensibly founded to search for truth, decision making based on what is currently fashionable should be anathema. The assumption here is that the way one creates change is through reasoned discourse, experimentation, validation, and consensus. The logic of one's argument should enable individuals to make rational decisions. Indeed, the fundamentals of the scientific mind require elaborate testing, review, and commentary before a decision is reached. If those scientists who we so admire in one arena are the architects of university reform, it should not be surprising that colleges and universities are slow to change and may seem resistant to innovation. Just as a medical doctor would not blithely try something new in an operating room that has not been adequately tested, that doctor-cum-professor is likely to be hesitant to change structures and processes that have worn well with time.

The best example of what some might think of as moribund institutions is what Burton Clark (1970) has labeled "distinctive colleges." Swarthmore, Reed, St. John's College, and Antioch were examples of distinctive colleges not only because they had a stand-apart curriculum but also because of an overarching ethos regarding how one acted in, and thought about, higher education. One irony of such institutions is that although they may seem decidedly countercultural—such as Reed or Antioch—they are also remarkably conservative with regard to change. St. John's College, for example, has a curriculum largely unchanged over the last 50 years; a visit to the campus bookstore today is not that different from a visit in 1960. Shelves of Greek literature are abundant, whereas evidence of current manias about pop culture are absent.

In a distinctive college where culture and ideology are dominant, resistance to change is particularly difficult. All of the institution's members think of the organization as theirs, so a concern for the structure, culture, and daily processes of the institution become paramount. When shared governance extends to all aspects of the institution, then what exists today presumably occurs for a particular reason. Changes will not only be resisted on fundamental aspects of the institution such as the curriculum but also on components that might be deemed trivial in other organizations, such as the food served in the dining hall or the personnel who account for custodial services.

If distinctive colleges are the prototype for how one defines a successful liberal arts institution, then words such as "entrepreneurial," "risk-taking," and "innovative" are viewed with suspicion. The point is not to innovate but to maintain what exists. And until recently, maintenance, from this perspective, has been thought of not only as ideologically correct but also economically prudent.

U.S. higher education came of age in the 20th century. If international rankings existed in the 19th century, barely a handful of American colleges or universities would have been considered world class. Today, more than half of the world's best institutions on every rankings table are located in the United States (Tierney & Lanford, 2017). A conundrum exists, then. On the one hand, America's postsecondary institutions are viewed as having seen better days; to keep doing the same thing is a recipe for disaster. Yet, on the other hand, our colleges and universities are thought of as the world's best. Nobel Prize awards commonly go to scientists who conduct research in the United States. Perhaps being considered a stick-in-the-mud is not so bad after all?

How is it possible that American higher education can be in dire need of innovation when by virtually every available method of analysis, America's postsecondary institutions are viewed as top in their class? One response is what worked in the past is not going to work in the future. There is a certain logic to such a response for some, but not all, of America's institutions. The cost of tuition has placed small liberal arts and regional colleges at greater risk today than a half-century ago; every few months another college announces its closure. A curriculum that extended leisurely over an academic year with a summer break for rest and rejuvenation (and to tend to the summer fields) is increasingly not of interest to students who have been raised on Twitter and streaming services that enable consumers to get an entire series in one sitting. In part, we agree with such an analysis. We would not be writing a book about innovation if our analysis was that postsecondary institutions did not need to change.

A counterintuitive response is to reject the label of colleges and universities as being resistant to change. The American professorate is more cited than faculty in any other country, and by every innovative measure—patents, intellectual property, start-ups, and the like—America's colleges and universities have been leading exemplars (Tijssen & Winnink, 2018). The manner in which one does research and scholarship today is night and day from the conduct of scholars only a generation ago.

Our own experience is useful. We have written this book without any paper passing between us, and frequently have written in real time as we trade drafts back and forth with one another. Even teaching, perhaps the function of a college most resistant to change, is different today from only a decade ago. Students regularly buy their textbooks online, and classes revolve around laptops and tablets. When we are away from campus, we are more likely to Zoom with a student than miss an appointment.

Which is it, then? Are universities like graveyards for innovation, or are they engines of reform? Are faculty stick-in-the-muds, or are they trainers for tomorrow's entrepreneurs? We answer these questions by arguing that the hallmarks of American higher education—academic freedom, tenure, shared governance, and institutional autonomy—are not inimical to innovation; rather, they remain crucial for an innovative environment.

All too often, however, a vulgar, even cynical, form of innovation suggests many of the primary tenets of the academy are the culprits that need to be eliminated. We shall further argue that organizational designs thoughtfully leveraging tenets such as academic freedom and shared governance need not be barriers to change. Instead, they have the potential to not only root the organization in its past but help propel it toward a prosperous future. They can draw on the respected talents and exceptional knowledge of individuals working in colleges and universities to innovate and implement lasting and impactful change strategies. Too often the discourse of innovation is framed around a neoliberal assumption that full-time employment rather than casual labor, or a shared structure for decision making, slows decisions down and needs to be eliminated. In what follows we disagree and elaborate on our reasoning for our disagreement.

Pillars or Roadblocks of Innovation?

We first offer our understanding of academic freedom, tenure, shared governance, and institutional autonomy, and then critique why they are currently under attack, in general, and particularly as impediments to innovation. We conclude with a defense of these tenets, as they historically have helped higher education institutions achieve excellence and remain relevant to society while stimulating innovation.

Understanding Academic Freedom

Academic freedom as an idea has existed for over a century in the United States. Graduate education in the late 19th century largely occurred in Europe for Americans who sought the academic life. They returned from their studies in Germany with the idea of *Lehrfreiheit*. The historian Frederick

Rudolph (1962) defined *Lehrfreiheit* as "the right of the university professor to freedom of inquiry and to freedom of teaching, the right to study and to report on [their] findings in an atmosphere of consent" (412). Young American faculty returned to their country with a desire to implement *Lehrfreiheit*, but the structures of university prevented change. Ironically, then, what today many see as an impediment to innovation was initially rejected because of the perceived import of the status quo.

Most historians of American higher education look to the late 19th century as the time when the modern university came into existence. Institutions such as Johns Hopkins, Cornell, Stanford, and the University of California at Berkeley all started after the Civil War. Research became a key component of academic life, and graduate education became central to elite institutions of higher learning. What had not changed was the administrative structure. The president and the board of trustees were the ones who made decisions about the institutions, and the faculty were little more than contractual employees. Indeed, more often than not, faculty had no contract and could be dismissed at will. The arrival of young PhDs from Europe desired more of a voice in the direction of the institution. The undertaking of research, coupled with the rapid rise of graduate education, suggested a greater role for faculty in the institution (Tierney & Lanford, 2014).

The professionalization of the faculty also enabled individuals to communicate with one another across campuses. By the start of the 20th century, knowledge production was beginning to coalesce around disciplines, and faculty had started professional organizations in order to communicate their findings with one another. Eventually, disciplinary associations saw a need for a pan-discipline organization that considered the needs of faculty writ large. The American Association of University Professors (AAUP) came into existence in 1915. Soon after its creation, the AAUP and its first president, John Dewey, had to consider multiple cases in which an individual's ability to speak their mind without fear of being fired were violated. The result was that the AAUP wrote a statement that codified the idea of academic freedom; many institutions followed suit by adopting the statement. In part, it read:

> The purpose of this statement is to promote public understanding and support of academic freedom and tenure and agreement upon procedures to ensure them in colleges and universities. Institutions of higher education are conducted for the common good and not to further the interest of either the individual teacher or the institution as a whole. The common good depends upon

the free speech for truth and its exposition. Academic freedom is essential to these purposes. (AAUP, 1940/1977)[1]

Since the time of the term's inception, academic freedom has been seen not only as a central idea of the academy but one that supported, rather than impeded, innovation. Academic freedom gave the faculty the right to investigate ideas without external interference. Rather than being told what to do, or to assume that some ideas ought not to be investigated, faculty had unfettered access to knowledge. The free range of ideas is precisely the kind of environment an accomplished professional desires to enable innovation.

UNDERSTANDING TENURE

If academic freedom was the idea, then tenure was the structure that enabled it to happen. Any organization needs to create structures and policies that implement the ideas and strategies of the participants. The AAUP came up with the idea of tenure not merely as job protection for their clientele but as a way to ensure that academic freedom would be protected. Tenure ensured that faculty had the time and ability to conduct research, to speak, to write, and to criticize without interference from either internal or external agents. Since their inception, tenure and academic freedom have been discussed and debated in the courts; the importance of academic freedom as an idea, and tenure as the structure that protects it, has been upheld. The Supreme Court, for example, has written that "our Nation is deeply committed to safeguarding academic freedom, which is of transcendent value to all of us and not merely to the teachers concerned. That freedom is therefore a special concern of the First Amendment, which does not tolerate laws that cause a pall of orthodoxy over the classroom" (*Keyishian v. Board of Regents of Univ. of State of N.Y.*, 1967).

The "transcendent value" of which the Supreme Court has written pertains to a commitment to democratic principles and free speech. The assumption of a capitalist society is that freedom enables good ideas to occur, and that in an academic organization the protection of that freedom is necessary because those ideas at times run contrary to the financial or political interests of one or another group—such as the university administration, an influential donor, or the state or national government. Rather than being seen as a structure that created a logjam in which deadwood was allowed to hang on, tenure was viewed as a vital component of creating and enabling an innovative organization. Indeed, by the end of the 20th century, virtually all legitimate nonprofit public and private postsecondary institutions in the United States had some form of tenure. To be sure, changes to the structure have taken place. Family-friendly policies, maternity leave, and longer probationary periods, as well as post-tenure review and a deeper analysis of which criteria should be employed in granting tenure, are examples of the sorts of changes that have been implemented. Nevertheless, at the start of the 21st century, the structure of tenure looked pretty much the way it looked a half-century earlier.

What has occurred, however, is the rapid elimination of individuals appointed to tenure-track positions. A generation ago, tenure-track hiring was more common, and part-time adjunct professors were largely confined to the professional schools such as education and law. Today, the opposite is true. Adjunct faculty account for the majority of hires regardless of institutional type. Part of the transformation has occurred because of the cost of tenure. Part-time labor is ostensibly cheaper than hiring a full-time employee who gets not only health and retirement benefits but also lifetime employment.

The transformation has occurred because many see tenure as an impediment to change. One assumption is that faculty are proverbial "stick-in-the-muds," and senior administrators know best about what to do. Whereas a century ago individuals viewed the university as a fountainhead for reform and creativity, today some individuals have come to the opposite conclusion—one that we obviously do not share. A point of concern for us is that many of the ideas being dismantled today, as we rush headlong to embrace an entrepreneurial environment, are the very ideas, structures, and processes that have made American higher education the envy of the world. We would be well advised to think thoughtfully before we drop something that has created such acclimation and envy. Why were tenure and academic freedom the vehicles for American greatness until the latter half of the 20th century but today are outmoded and in need of radical reform, if not abandonment? We are concerned that the answer has less to do with creating an innovative environment and more with two desires: (1) a top-down organization where management controls the conditions of work and (2) political and corporate control over faculty who conduct research and teach curricula that pose thoughtful, evidence-based challenges to powerful vested interests. This is a concern we will return to in our final chapter.

A second point of concern is where tenure and academic freedom do not exist is in organizations that are the "newest kids on the block"—which are frequently for-profit colleges and universities. Institutions such as the University of Phoenix and DeVry University managed enormous growth in the late 20th and early 21st centuries. Unfortunately, they also demonstrated practices that harmed students and cost taxpayers hundreds of million dollars because of deceptive practices (Cottom, 2017; Shireman, 2017; Shireman & Cochrane, 2017). One comment frequently made is that non-profit higher education needs to be "nimbler," like the for-profits. One can reasonably ask if such agility is what one wants to mimic if it has been found to be a swamp of scurrilous practices. Perhaps management does not always know best.

UNDERSTANDING SHARED GOVERNANCE

The creation of the AAUP, the concept of academic freedom, and the structure of tenure in many respects led to the incarnation of shared governance as an additional central concept of American higher education. Prior to the 20th century, governance was thin and largely held by the president. By the middle of the 20th century, a transformation had occurred. Obviously, if decisions about tenure needed to be made, and the basis was made upon the quality of a professor's work, then a simple administrative position was impossible. Instead, those who knew best about the quality of specific areas of inquiry needed to offer judgments about a candidate; thus, faculty had an obvious voice in who worked in the institution.

We mentioned above that, within a year of its founding, the AAUP had multiple requests for help and advice from individuals who believed that academic freedom had been violated on their campuses. The investigations led to analyses where administrative interference was substantial, and the faculty voice was muted, and of consequence, the faculty's role in governance acquired strength. Academic Senates came of age in the middle of the century, and the assumption was taken for granted that faculty participated in the future of the institution (Gerber, 2014).

Context matters as well. Throughout the early 20th century, and well into the second half of the century, unionization was on the rise. American higher education, however, largely eschewed the ideology that the workers needed representation. Instead, the more genteel idea of shared governance took hold. Colleges and universities did not always need unions for faculty because the faculty were involved in the governance of the institution. Shared governance had commonalities with the idea of the protection of workers' rights. To be sure, shared governance had more to do with the protection of academic freedom, but over time other topics, such as rights and benefits, became important issues as well. That is, what a professor taught and how they investigated issues that may be controversial certainly were logical areas for faculty to invoke concerns about academic freedom. However, as the salaries and benefits of the administration rose and the salaries of tenured faculty froze or eroded, there was a growing awareness that tenure was meaningless, or at least weakened, if the salaries did not provide the ability to live a comfortable middle-class life.

External agents also accepted the notion that shared governance was not only a useful idea but a critical one. Regional and professional accreditation agencies all required institutions to have an elaborated governance structure that included the faculty. State legislatures either required or accepted the fact of shared governance with regard to state appropriations. Funding agencies also frequently wanted to know how the faculty was involved in decision making on a campus.

Although shared governance had its origins with regard to academic freedom, the evolution of the academy also contributed to what might be seen as natural. The AAUP's initial statements argued that faculty ought to be able to pursue truth, wherever it may lead, not only with regard to their research and teaching but also on their campuses. If one accepts such a statement, then virtually any aspect of campus life is open for faculty commentary. Recognize that in "distinctive colleges" the result was that faculty would be involved in virtually every aspect of academic life. In some instances, such an interpretation meant representation on the board of trustees. On most campuses, however, the protection of shared governance coupled with tenure enabled faculty to criticize the president and senior administration, or to raise extramural comments from their primary intellectual areas, and not face sanction.

At the same time, however, the academy increased the rigor and scope of its areas of investigation, and they relied on the free labor of the academy. If national and state agencies were to provide funding for research, and the quality of proposals needed to be reviewed, then the faculty were the natural experts to call on to make scholarly recommendations. The increase in academic journals and the professionalization of disciplinary associations required free labor from academics, if associations were to get their jobs done. On college and university campuses, numerous committees needed the participation of academics in order to function. On the one hand, one might see all of this involvement as a remarkable service by the professoriate, who spent a good deal of their working lives undertaking tasks for free.

On the other hand, as the 20th century ended, many critics looked to this elaborate structure as antithetical to the creation of an innovative climate for conducting one's research. Just as one criticizes the federal government for too much regulation, the oversight that exists on college campuses where multiple committees dominated by academics review various proposals could be viewed as obstructing, rather than encouraging, innovation. What needed to occur, from this perspective, was (at a minimum) a lessening, or even an elimination, of shared governance. As with academic freedom and tenure, the critics largely dismissed the past and the acknowledgment that higher education had become great through a shared governance structure. The critics simply looked at the present logjams that existed on campuses and put forward ideas on how to ramp up entrepreneurial activity. The result was a reduction in shared governance and the voice of the faculty.

Understanding Institutional Autonomy

The final pillar of the 20th-century academy that has come under attack is institutional autonomy. One might assume that for an innovative environment to prosper autonomy might be seen as a positive. Who needs all those governmental regulations and oversight? An irony is that, as governmental fiscal support has decreased, the clamor for greater oversight of nonprofit public and private higher education has increased (Alexander, 2000; Suspitsyna, 2010).

Although the AAUP initially had very little to say about the structural autonomy of postsecondary institutions, over time, in the twentieth century, the assumption became belief that universities should be largely self-regulated. Yes, states appropriated revenue to institutions, and funding agencies provided an assortment of loans, grants and financial support for buildings, research, and infrastructure. However, the assumption was largely that those who knew the best about the institution were those who worked within the institution—and the faculty were a significant part of the decision-making apparatus. Again, a great deal of the "hands-off" attitude toward the academy was also that the reputation of colleges and universities was sky-rocketing. It was hard to argue that greater regulation should be put in place around colleges and universities when they appeared to be doing everything right. Foreign students clamored to our shores. Enrollments continued apace. Faculty won prestigious awards. Some of the most admired individuals in America were professors. What was not to like?

The faculty might be viewed as the culprits. In the closing decades of the 20th century, American higher education received very favorable commentary from the public, writ large. The increasingly vocal and powerful conservative movement in the United States had a different analysis. Our institutions were breeding grounds for radical thought that undermined democracy. The 1960s, for some, were a time of social and cultural upheaval that was aided and abetted by the faculty. The faculty were largely liberal, even radical, and had an agenda that ran contrary to the definition of democracy as put forward by conservatives (Himmelstein & Zald, 1984).

The best way to control academic institutions was to look to their funding sources. Thus, even as states reduced financial support, they increased oversight. A concern for very real issues—completion rates, time to degree, admissions policies—were certainly a problem, but as we have previously noted, one cannot divorce organizational life from the environment in which it finds itself. Ironically, at the same time that governmental regulation was being reduced at for-profit colleges and universities, the clamor was to reduce the autonomy of traditional higher education. The intent was to ensure that institutions were more in line with governmental prerogatives, rather than simply doing whatever the faculty desired. And, in this case, the critique had little to do with innovation or creativity. Few analysts saw the irony: for those who called for the lessening of regulation so that the market might rule, and innovation might be unchained, the exact opposite calls have been made about colleges and universities.

Our point here is straightforward. American higher education came of age in the 20th century and became the envy of the world. The scaffolding for greatness—academic freedom, tenure, shared governance, and institutional autonomy—are now what critics deride. As Simon Waxman (2012) has noted, innovation "is a loaded word. It does a great deal of work, painting a vast landscape of meanings even as it obliterates or camouflages others" (2). Innovation is portrayed by some almost like a magic elixir with no normative content. What concerns us is that innovation is often put forward without a recognition of where we are heading or why, almost as if any change is fine because the status quo must be blown apart.

Innovation is not a neutral, nonideological concept. While we fully support the idea that postsecondary institutions need to change, we also recognize that far too often those who call for changes are advocating ruptures to the very fabric of higher education's greatness. What we wish to foreground here is the realization that calls for innovation frequently mask attempts to defrock higher education and bifurcate institutional purpose, strategy, and ideology from action. What is really going on with the rhetoric of entrepreneurialism is an attempt to de-politicize the academy for those who worry about the work of academics while simultaneously eliminating any sense of civic purpose to the academic enterprise. In effect, the attempt seems to be not merely to implement steps to make an organization more innovative but to entirely remake the academy so that it is entirely market oriented and acquiescent to political and corporate interests. If such an attempt is successful, innovative progress will grind to a resounding halt and previously respected higher educations will become inert organizations dominated by sterile curricula and ineffectual scholarship. This might be the type of environment desired by a totalitarian regime, but it has no utility in a democratic society.

Building the Conditions for Mindful Innovation on History and Precedent

Our focus here has been to point out that frequently, although not always, the call for innovation has either been an explicit rejection of the core pillars of academic life or a more implicit understanding that an innovative organization is one that rejects the past rather than builds on it. We are concerned that a headlong rush in the pursuit of innovation has the potential of eliminating that which has made American higher education the envy of the world. The empirical evidence does not demonstrate that, to create an innovative environment, one needs to discard the past.

How, then, might one proceed? We are suggesting that rather than discredit and throw overboard the reformist efforts being undertaken by innovative professors and administrators, we embrace radical changes that nevertheless vigorously support the university's role in strengthening civil society. In the next chapter we will lay out the contours of how we see innovation working in higher education. None of what we write there suggests that academic freedom must be eliminated or casual labor must be the norm. Further, we will point out how teamwork and collaboration needs to be the norm, rather than a top-down management style. As de Souza Santos (2010) has cogently argued, we must offer an alternative analysis that enables our understanding of the "counter-hegemonic globalization of the university as a public good that means the national reform of the [public] university [will be] . . . centered on policy choices that consider the country's insertion in increasingly transnational contexts of knowledge production and distribution" (5). And as a public good, sensible regulation of higher education ought to be the norm rather than fought.

The problem with many management-focused remedies for higher education is that one's analysis gets intertwined with an ideological focus aimed at stifling, rather than promoting, creativity. Perhaps in what sociologist Erving Goffman (1961/1977) has described as "total institutions," many suggestions that have put been forward make sense. Organizations such as the military need to evolve and change, and innovation ought to be embraced rather than rejected. But what makes the military successful is antithetical to what has made academic life a success. Colleges and universities do not have generals, and there is no reason to think that absolute commanders make sense in higher education.

A challenge for those of us committed to making academe more innovative is not to call for innovation as an abstraction but to be clear about what ails higher education and then consider what creative solutions might be. When we look at different colleges and universities, we are not suggesting that they innovate for innovation's sake; the purpose of innovation is to make the organization truer to its mission and ideals, rather than an abandonment of those ideals. As Sotiris (2014) usefully argues, "We need to move from the idea of the university to an attempt to actually theorize its role and the potential for resistance within it. . . . It is not enough to theorize" (5). Understanding academic life and applying the principles we have put forward for mindful innovation ought to enable higher education to move forward in the critical mission that society expects of us.

Chapter 9

Moving Forward with a
Culture of Mindful Innovation

To reiterate the main points of this book, in Chapter 2 we delineated how three conditions are challenging traditional roles within higher education. First, the contemporary vision of the knowledge economy has become central to workforce development and economic forecasting. Second, the rapid development of technological and computerized systems is likely to have a profound and lasting impact on future labor markets. Third, higher education is massifying throughout the world while, concurrently, institutions compete to develop recognizable brands on the global stage and government funding for higher education is being cut in many regions of the world. The confluence of these developments could limit access to colleges and universities and catalyze even greater competitive pressure between institutions.

In Chapter 3 we argued that disruptive innovation theory may be useful for identifying emerging technologies that could upend the teaching and learning aspects of higher education. It could also help individuals imagine how a potentially innovative product might transform over time and gain mass acceptance within a specific field. However, we think it is an ill-suited theory for predicting higher education's transformation in the 21st century. Our argument was based on an analysis of the ideological reasons behind the promotion of disruptive innovation and the lack of empirical evidence for disruption in higher education—and in other sectors ostensibly transformed by disruption. We are thus quite concerned that individuals will prematurely disrupt the vital functions of otherwise successful colleges and universities by relying on "disruption" as a scare tactic, rather than acknowledging the need for a mindful consideration of existing institutional cultures and the fundamental limitations of disruptive innovation as a theory.

In Chapter 4 we criticized the fundamental assumptions behind New Public Management. We demonstrated how they distill complex institutional missions into simplistic conversations about efficiency and effectiveness, and these trends not only run counter to effective governance but to the promotion of creativity and innovation. Colleges and universities, by necessity, have multiple missions, such as workforce development, research into societal problems, the advancement of disciplinary knowledge, and community service. These missions are central to higher education, and we believe they require a multifaceted conceptualization of innovation incongruent with the simplistic celebrations of privatization, performance funding, and cost reduction by acolytes of neoliberalism and New Public Management.

Hence, in Chapter 5 we conceptualized creativity, innovation, and entrepreneurship through a multidisciplinary lens that attempted to do justice to higher education's vast diversity of individuals, mission statements, and areas of scholarly inquiry. We showed how both *creativity* and *entrepreneurship* overlap with *innovation* in specific ways. Creativity refers to inventiveness grounded in field-specific knowledge and expedited by motivation. Innovation pertains to the implementation of a creative product or process and its perceived novelty once it has been evaluated by a critical audience. While creativity is a necessary condition for innovative thinking, not all creative individuals or organizations have been innovative. Meanwhile, entrepreneurship is largely motivated by the prospects for financial growth. Entrepreneurial strategies often rely on innovation, but innovative thinking is not always motivated, or even induced, by entrepreneurial objectives.

With these concepts defined, we then specified in Chapter 6 four environmental factors that stimulate mindful innovation: diversity, intrinsic motivation, autonomy, and creative conflict. Chapter 7 focused on three dimensions—time, efficiency, and trust—that impact the adoption, development, and implementation of innovation. Chapter 7 also contended that the institutional fit, potential impact, and likelihood of longevity of any innovation should be thoughtfully considered by institutions before diffusion is attempted.

Finally, in Chapter 8 we countered prevailing public discourse by arguing that American higher education is a remarkable success story viewed by other countries as worthy of emulation. Clearly, not all of its traditions should be discarded. In particular, four important tenets of American higher education—academic freedom, tenure, shared governance, and institutional autonomy—have proven to be indispensable in fostering a creative intellectual environment that can result in innovative progress. A discussion of these tenets was embedded in a critique of the shortcomings of contemporary rhetoric on innovation.

Thus, we now come full circle, returning to Chapter 1 and how we demarcated our approach to mindful innovation at the opening of the book. Mindful innovation is summarized through six central tenets that resonate with our arguments in each chapter. These tenets include (1) societal impact; (2) the necessity of failure; (3) creativity through diversity; (4) respect for autonomy and expertise; (5) the consideration of time, efficiency, and trust; and (6) the incentivization of intrinsic motivation and progress over scare tactics and disruption.

In longer form, we contend that a mindful approach to innovation has the following qualities:

1. A focus on the *societal impact*, as well as the entrepreneurial potential, of any potential innovation, especially for traditionally marginalized groups.

2. A welcoming environment for experimentation that critically examines *failure* as a part of the innovation process.

3. The promotion of *creativity through diversity* by bringing together groups that represent a broad and diverse spectrum of experiences, backgrounds, and content areas.

4. A safeguarding of individual *autonomy* and respect for *expertise* through venerable institutional and personal protections, such as academic freedom, shared governance, tenure, and institutional independence.

5. A thorough and rigorous consideration of the dimensions of *time, efficiency, and trust*—and their impact on the adoption, development, and implementation of any innovation.

6. Incentives that stimulate the *intrinsic motivation* of individuals and organizations invested in innovative *progress*, rather than the promulgation of scare tactics that warn of impending disruption.

By offering these tenets, we want to encourage leaders of institutions, policymakers, and practitioners within higher education institutions to be more measured and thoughtful in their approach to innovation. Most importantly, we want to reshift the focus on innovation from the expeditious creation of potentially disruptive ideas that are walled off from society. Instead, we believe that colleges and universities must actively cultivate healthy institutional cultures that incubate innovations while maintaining a long-term perspective and sharing accrued knowledge in the spirit of transparency and growth.

Where Do We Go from Here?

Contrary to many other innovation acolytes, we resist the creation of a cookbook with instructions for what higher education should do moving forward, as if a simple list of ingredients could yield a recipe for innovation. And yet, we recognize that much of our argument to this point may seem theoretical for those looking for more prescriptive measures. Accordingly, we would like to conclude this book with eight ideas that warrant review and summarization here.

1. **Acknowledge that change is needed.** Different constituencies see issues from their own perspective, and that is not necessarily bad. But all too often senior leadership has access to a great deal of data through which they reach an objective conclusion that the institution faces trouble and change must occur. Unfortunately, they frequently have not taken the time to be mindful of how others view the environment. The provost may see that classes over the last decade have slipped from 20 students to 15 students and is painfully aware of how that results in lost revenue. As instructors, we have not seen a very big dip in change because the drop has been gradual, and we are working just as hard as ever.

For innovation to succeed, the entire community must understand the challenges that exist in order for a creative environment to be enacted. Critics will charge that communication is too time consuming and reverts to the stasis that they want to avoid. We counter that for an innovate climate to be sustainable, there needs to be buy-in not simply by a few senior administrators but across the board. The strategy called for here is unceasing communication that not only seeks to set the stage for change but also solicits input from diverse populations about how they interpret the problems that exist and what sorts of solutions might be brought forward. Communication also is not sporadic or made at the beginning of the school year. Communication is dialogical and ongoing.

2. Define what's central to colleges and universities. Nonprofit institutions are fundamentally different from for-profit organizations, and we suggest that colleges and universities are also distinct within the nonprofit world. Indeed, Burton Clark (1970) once defined a subset of postsecondary institutions as "distinctive" because the organization's members had an investment in multiple aspects of the organization and a deep identification with the institution's saga. Although most organizations have much greater leeway than distinctive colleges, all institutions have some values that inform an institution's culture.

Companies try to create affiliations with their customers, and they try to brand the organization in a specific manner. The question to ask here is, what are those values and ideologies that define our institution? We have made a strong case that academic freedom is certainly a core value for many, but not all, postsecondary institutions. We also have pointed out how tenure is the structure that supports the value. One cannot make the facile claim to support academic freedom but eliminate tenure. Words have to be supported by actions. We certainly appreciate that changes may require adjustments in staffing, but we caution against disruptions that will destroy an institution's core values.

Core values are core. They are not a laundry list. They are not shared by some but ignored by others. Core values give the organization an identity and organizing framework. Rather than limiting change, a mindful organization sees core values as the scaffolding that facilitates dramatic change while maintaining a distinctive identity.

3. Define the environment for the institution. Environments are enacted (Chafee & Tierney, 1988). How an organization defines its environment is not merely a geographic question. Some regional institutions define "region" in a manner very differently from others. Defining the environment is also not simply an issue that should be left up to the admissions and marketing departments. We fully appreciate that in tuition-driven institutions individuals will seek to change their environment if there is a paucity in the yield of students from their traditional environment. Changing the environment is particularly tempting in schools that call upon a single sort of constituency (e.g., women, religious denominations).

By no means do we believe that the geography that defined the past must define the future. But we do believe that a clear determination needs to be made and shared about the sorts of environment in which the organization will exist. What we urge caution about, however, is the assumption that the world is the environment for an organization. Foreign students are a viable market, and online learning opens up markets that may never before have been considered. But foreign students bring their own distinct issues that can certainly enhance a community's learning environment if handled consciously, rather than being seen as simply another "yield" to meet the revenue goal.

By many institutions, online learning was once considered an economic savior. However, it has proven to be an expensive undertaking with many hidden costs related to course design; the integration of new learning platforms; online marketing; and the employment of web designers, multimedia specialists, virtual student support staff, and data analysts; in fact, a study by state officials in Florida found that online coursework cost approximately $41 per credit hour more than in-person coursework (Newton, 2018). Therefore, online learning may not solve every institution's fiscal problems. The limitations of virtual learning—from a lack of internet access for students in rural areas to missed deadlines and reduced opportunities for social connections—have also become all too apparent during the Covid-19 pandemic (Adedoyin & Soykan, 2021; Chan, Bista, & Allen, 2021). What is most important for our purposes here is a philosophical rationale consistent with the organization's culture for how students are to be taught and how they are to learn. Mindful innovation posits that one is not simply doing a rote task but that one is aware of the environment in which we exist and how we accomplish our work.

4. Embrace constructive critique and shared governance. Some innovation proponents work from a perspective that innovation either just happens or that the organization needs strong leaders who direct the change. We are not commenting on the viability of such advice in other organizations, but we take issue with such an approach in a postsecondary institution. Indeed, another central value of academic life—and one that came of age at the same time that America's predominance in higher education came about—is the idea of shared governance. We certainly acknowledge that different constituencies will have different perspectives on academic life—but rather than try to subjugate or avoid differences, a mindful approach will embrace the constructive critique enabled by shared governance. Disagreements need not slow down decision making, but those involved do need to be aware of the sorts of time constraints that exist and facilitate structured decision making. From this perspective, an innovative organization is one where agreement exists on what sorts of values the college or university holds, and where a plan is developed to aggressively pursue ideas that have been vetted and debated by the community.

5. Encourage independent, critical feedback. This argument is related to the previous point on constructive critique. For a culture of mindful innovation, there should be space for critical feedback not only in the planning stage but also throughout the implementation and diffusion phases. The inclination to portray every development with an emerging innovation in a positive light is understandable since investments in innovation, especially technological innovations, are generally quite expensive. Nevertheless, such an attitude inexorably leads to skepticism and resistance among those in higher education who hold considerable expertise in their fields. Often, the primary question surrounding the adoption of a technological innovation in higher education, for instance, is whether the sunk investments come at the cost of viable alternatives, such as hiring more full-time academic support staff or offering childcare services, that might be more effective. It is incumbent on institutions to mindfully reflect on these types of issues, rather than cheerlead, if an innovation is to have any semblance of legitimacy.

A series of questions that a healthy culture of mindful innovation might ask include the following:

1. In which ways did/could the innovative framework or innovative project fail, or at least struggle to meet expectations?

2. How could elements of the innovative framework or project be refined in the future?

3. Who might be negatively impacted by the adoption and diffusion of this innovation? For what reasons?

4. What are the limitations of this innovation?

Without this critical inquiry—and a transparent accounting for potential negative outcomes—many knowledgeable and well-intentioned individuals will be cynical about the innovation's purported impact and future direction.

6. Emphasize outreach. One change from the past is that our ivy-covered institutions need to be much more aggressive in various sorts of outreach to their local and regional communities. The type of outreach depends on the kind of institution and its mission, as well as the environment and its needs. For most of their history, postsecondary institutions have been inward looking. To be sure, they still need to pay attention to internal processes and actors, but part of innovation is engagement with diverse communities in ways perhaps not yet envisioned.

We appreciate that innovations do not necessarily have to involve external agents. But we are suggesting here that an innovative organization is one that does not wall itself off from local communities and external constituencies. A climate for innovation suggests that individuals have a sense of the sorts of changes that other constituencies may need, and an idea about with whom to collaborate for change. Such a suggestion, while appearing modest, actually has the potential for changing a great many policies and procedures about the sorts of incentives that might be created to encourage engagement with one's community. Previously, most work incentives focused on what one did within the institution; we are reframing the idea to incentivize action outside the institution.

7. Understand when students are customers and when they are students. We appreciate that using the idea that students are customers runs the risk of falling into a neoliberal framework. At their core, students are students, and an innovative organization is one where learning experiences are created that are mindful of the sorts of activities, in and out of class, that enable deeper engagement. An innovative college or university certainly must develop learning activities that call upon the newest technologies and advances in understanding how individuals learn. But mindful innovation is not simply buying things such as iPads. We are troubled, too, that students routinely skip classes because they can find class notes posted to the web or get them from a friend. If the classroom is no longer a learning environment in which existing knowledge is questioned and preconceived ideas are challenged, then in our "instruction" we are doing little more than engaging in a charade. Instead, we need creative innovations that meet the needs of today's student while encouraging growth through interrogation and inquiry.

When we employ the idea of students as customers, we are simply acknowledging that the organization does need to change its mindset (Chaffee & Tierney, 1988). Classes and academic life have all too frequently been arranged around a professor's schedule. For-profit higher education certainly made egregious errors—but they also had some good ideas. FPCUs structured class times and locations around the needs of their students. Public and private institutions would be well advised to foster that mindset as well. Students also are media savvy. Certainly, many institutions have made admirable progress in this regard. Registration was once a day-long event in the campus gym, or involved a marathon series of phone calls. Thankfully, the majority of students can now register online at their convenience. Getting a book from the campus library was once an adventure with the Dewey Decimal system as your guide. Today, books and articles can be viewed online—a saving grace during the recent pandemic. These sorts of customer-based changes need to continue as the organization develops innovative ways to more closely meet the practical, social, and academic needs of their various constituencies.

8. Focus on agreed-on outcomes. Mindful innovation sets goals. The goals are in sync with the mission of the organization and agreed on by the organization's members. To be sure, the scholar doing research in a laboratory, or a writer engaged in writing a text, may have creativity as a framework, which the organization wants to enable. But, for the organization itself, goals need to be established that create and facilitate innovation and organizational well-being. On the one hand, we need to come to grips with how to enable those academics to have an innovative climate. On the other hand, we need to be aware of the goals for the organization and how they might be reached.

Further, it is important to reiterate that creativity is not simply an individual trait that some possess and others do not. Likewise, innovation within an organization is not simply organic, or something that just "happens." Organizations have the potential to nurture creativity in their members and enable innovative climates. To do so, however, an organization's leaders need to be strategic.

In summary, we believe action sparked by a crisis mentality—or driven by the notion that things must be disrupted—is far from optimal. Instead, when considering their actions, decision makers should carefully consider an institution's history, its culture, and its strengths and weaknesses relative to its peers and emerging innovative forces. Rather than adhere to processes that lack empirical evidence for their efficacy or may have worked a generation ago, colleges and universities should foster conditions that reward intrinsic motivation, autonomy, and diversity—and take into account the temporal conditions that lead to successful organizational change. Such a framework requires internally derived assessment measures that focus attention on creative inquiry and innovative discovery, not externally derived measures that promote conformity. Through such deliberate and informed choices, an institution can strategically build a culture that actively nurtures creativity and innovation—and that leads to greater social equity and scientific progress.

Notes

Chapter 1

1. Portions of Chapters 5, 6, and 7 appeared previously in the following sources: "Cultivating Strategic Innovation in Higher Education": www.tiaainstitute. org/publication/cultivating-strategic-innovation and "Conceptualizing Innovation in Higher Education": https://doi.org/10.1007/978-3-319-26829-3_1

Chapter 2

1. See www.treasury.gov/resource-center/data-chart-center/Documents/2012 0413_FinancialCrisisResponse.pdf.

2. See www.uspto.gov/web/offices/ac/ido/oeip/taf/us_stat.pdf.

3. See www.federalreserve.gov/boarddocs/speeches/2002/200209252/default. htm.

4. See http://whitepapers.stern.nyu.edu/summaries/ch10.html.

5. See www.youtube.com/watch?time_continue=191&v=TWSRgsk2oaw.

6. See https://nces.ed.gov/programs/coe/indicator_cac.asp.

7. We avoid the terms "traditional" and "non-traditional" as they are increasingly considered erroneous, non-inclusive, and harmful in today's higher education environment. For example, see Needham Gulley's article, "The Myth of the Nontraditional Student," at www.insidehighered.com/views/2016/08/05/defining-students-nontraditional-inaccurate-and-damaging-essay.

8. See www.schoolcounselor.org/getmedia/b079d17d-6265-4166-a120-3b1f56077649/School-Counselors-Matter.pdf.

9. See https://edsource.org/2020/how-some-california-school-districts-invest-in-counseling-and-achieve-results/623489.

Chapter 3

1. These states are Alabama, Arizona, California, Colorado, Florida, Georgia, Hawaii, and Louisiana.

2. See www.brookings.edu/blog/up-front/2021/02/12/putting-student-loan-forgiveness-in-perspective-how-costly-is-it-and-who-benefits.

3. For a comprehensive—and recent—discussion of the public good and higher education, see the following article: S. Marginson (2018), Public/private in higher education: A synthesis of economic and political approaches, *Studies in Higher Education*, *43*(2), 322–337.

4. See www.ucop.edu/institutional-research-academic-planning/_files/affordability_at_uc.pdf.

5. For a graph of real median household income in the United States since 1988, see https://fred.stlouisfed.org/series/MEHOINUSA672N.

6. See "Student Loans" under "Consumer Credit Outstanding (Levels)" on the following Federal Reserve Statistics website: www.federalreserve.gov/releases/g19/current/default.htm.

7. Our discussion of these issues is updated from our monograph for the TIAA Institute entitled *Cultivating Strategic Innovation in Higher Education* at www.tiaainstitute.org/publication/cultivating-strategic-innovation.

8. Ibid.

9. Joshua Kim and Edward Maloney (2020) provide a much more comprehensive history concerning the development of MOOCs, dating back to the 2008 experiments of George Siemens at Athabasca University and Stephen Downes at the National Research Council of Canada. Their text is also highly recommended for a compelling discussion of learning innovation as an emerging interdisciplinary field of study and for its advocacy of nuanced organizational change.

10. See https://littlebylittlejohn.com/professional-learning-in-moocs. Also see A. Littlejohn & N. Hood (2018), *Reconceptualizing learning in the digital age: The [un]democratizing potential of MOOCs*. Springer.

Chapter 5

1. See www.ucop.edu/president/public-engagement/usc-pullias-feb-2015.html.

2. See https://stevens.usc.edu.

3. See www.annenberglab.com.

4. See http://viterbi.usc.edu/innovation.

5. See http://iovine-young.usc.edu.

6. See www.gainesville.com/article/20150328/ARTICLES/150329629?tc=ar.

7. See www.gainesville.com/article/20140327/articles/140329618.

8. See www.cbpp.org/research/states-are-still-funding-higher-education-below-pre-recession-levels.

9. See www.washingtonpost.com/blogs/answer-sheet/wp/2015/04/06/university-of-florida-admits-3000-students-then-tells-them-it-is-only-for-online-program.

10. See www.recsports.ufl.edu/facilities/student-recreation-fitness-center.

11. Also see WGU 2018 Annual Report at www.wgu.edu/content/dam/western-governors/documents/annual-report/annual-report-2018.pdf.

Chapter 6

1. We have not participated in one of the design-thinking seminars offered by the Stanford School. Our critique is thus limited to the basic outline of the theory rather than firsthand practice.

2. Unfortunately, as of the publication of this book, such reforms were being rolled back in Hong Kong due to perceptions that liberal arts education inspired antigovernment protests. See, for example, www.scmp.com/news/hong-kong/education/article/3102439/what-liberal-studies-hong-kong-and-why-it-controversial.

3. For more information, see the forthcoming article here: https://doi.org/10.1080/00131857.2020.1783246.

4. See www.nytimes.com/2015/08/16/technology/inside-amazon-wrestling-big-ideas-in-a-bruising-workplace.html.

5. See, for example, www.timeshighereducation.co.uk/410297.article. Also see http://theconversation.com/collegiality-is-dead-in-the-new-corporatised-university-5539.

Chapter 8

1. See www.aaup.org/report/1940-statement-principles-academic-freedom-and-tenure.

References

Abel, J. R., & Deitz, R. (2014). Do the benefits of college still outweigh the costs? *Current Issues in Economics and Finance*, *20*(3), 1–12.

Acharya, V. V., Brenner, M., Engle, R., Lynch, A., & Richardson, M. (2009). Derivatives—the ultimate financial innovation. In V. V. Acharya & M. Richardson (Eds.), *Restoring financial stability: How to repair a broken system* (pp. 233–250). Wiley.

Ackermann, M. (2013). The communication of innovation—An empirical analysis of the advancement of innovation (Discussion paper). Discussion Papers on Strategy and Innovation. Philipps-University Marburg. http://www.econstor.eu/bitstream/10419/77064/1/751413305.pdf

Adams, R., Bessant, J., & Phelps, R. (2006). Innovation management measurement: A review. *International Journal of Management Reviews*, *8*(1), 21–47.

Adedoyin, O. B., & Soykan, E. (2021). Covid-19 pandemic and online learning: The challenges and opportunities. *Interactive Learning Environments*. Advance online publication. https://doi.org/10.1080/10494820.2020.1813180

Adler, K. (2021). IHS markit forecasts global ev sales to rise by 70% in 2021. IHS Markit. https://ihsmarkit.com/research-analysis/ihs-markit-forecasts-global-ev-sales-to-rise-by-70-percent.html

Alexander, F. K. (2000). The changing face of accountability: Monitoring and assessing institutional performance in higher education. *Journal of Higher Education*, *71*(4), 411–431.

Allen, I. E., & Seaman, J. (2013). Changing course: Ten years of tracking online education in the United States. Babson Survey Research Group. http://files.eric.ed.gov/fulltext/ED541571.pdf

Altbach, P. G., & Hazelkorn, E. (2017). Pursing rankings in the age of massification: For most—forget about it. *International Higher Education*, *89*, 8–10.

Altbach, P. G., Reisberg, L., & de Wit, H. (Eds.). (2017). *Responding to massification: Differentiation to postsecondary education worldwide*. Sense Publishers.

Alves, M. G., & Tomlinson, M. (2021). The changing value of higher education in England and Portugal: Massification, marketization, and public good. *European Educational Research Journal, 20*(2), 176–192.

Amabile, T. M. (1998). How to kill creativity. *Harvard Business Review, 76*, 77–87.

Amabile, T. M., Barsade, S. G., Mueller, J. S., & Staw, B. M. (2005). Affect and creativity at work. *Administrative Science Quarterly, 50*, 367–403.

Amabile, T. M., Conti, R., Coon, H., Lazenby, J., & Herron, M. (1996). Assessing the work environment for creativity. *Academy of Management Journal, 39*(5), 1154–1184.

Amabile, T. M., Hadley, C. N., & Kramer, S. J. (2002). Creativity under the gun. *Harvard Business Review, 80*(8), 52–61.

American Association of University Professors (AAUP). (2018). Data snapshot: Contingent faculty in U.S. higher ed. https://www.aaup.org/sites/default/files/10112018%20Data%20Snapshot%20Tenure.pdf

Angulo, A. J. (2016). *Diploma mills: How for-profit colleges stiffed students, taxpayers, and the American dream.* Johns Hopkins University Press.

Arce, E., & Segura, D. A. (2015). Stratification in the labor market. In J. Stone, R. M. Dennis, P. S. Rizova, A. D. Smith, & X. Hou (Eds.), *The Wiley Blackwell encyclopedia of race, ethnicity, and nationalism.* Wiley.

Armona, L., Chakrabarti, R., & Lovenheim, M. (2018). How does for-profit college attendance affect student loans, defaults, and labor market outcomes? (FRB of NY Staff Report No. 811). Federal Reserve Bank of New York.

Arnett, P. (1968). Major describes move. *New York Times.*

Arnove, R. (2003). Introduction: Reframing comparative education: The dialectic of the global and the local. In R. Arnove and C. A. Torres (Eds.), *Comparative Education: The dialectic of the global and the local.* Rowman and Littlefield.

Autor, D., & Dorn, D. (2013). The growth of low-skill service jobs and the polarization of the U.S. labor market. *American Economic Review, 103*(5), 1553–1597.

Autor, D., Katz, L. F., & M. S. Kearney. (2006). The polarization of the U.S. labor market. American Economic Review, 96(2), 189–194.

Autor, D., & Reynolds, E. (2020). *The nature of work after the COVID crisis: Too few low-wage jobs.* Brookings. https://www.hamiltonproject.org/assets/files/AutorReynolds_LO_FINAL.pdf

Baer, R. A. (2003). Mindfulness training as a clinical intervention: A conceptual and empirical review. *Clinical Psychology: Science and Practice, 10*(2), 125–143.

Barber, N. (2016). The film *Star Wars* stole from. *BBC Culture.* https://www.bbc.com/culture/article/20160104-the-film-star-wars-stole-from

Baregheh, A., Rowley, J., & Sambrook, S. (2009). Towards a multidisciplinary definition of innovation. *Management Decision, 47*(8), 1323–1339.

Barnichon, R., Matthes, C., & Ziegenbein, A. (2018). The financial crisis at 10: Will we ever recover? Federal Reserve Bank of San Francisco. https://www.frbsf.org/economic-research/publications/economic-letter/2018/august/financial-crisis-at-10-years-will-we-ever-recover

Barnshaw, J., & Dunietz, S. (2015). Busting the myths: The annual report on the economic status of the profession, 2014–15. *Academe, 101*(2), 4–19.

Baum, S. (2015). The evolution of student debt in the United States. In B. Hershbein & K. M. Hollenbeck (Eds.), *Student loans and the dynamics of debt* (pp. 11–35). Upjohn Institute for Employment Research.

Baumol, W. J., & Bowen, W. G. (1966). *Performing arts, the economic dilemma: A study of problems common to theater, opera, music, and dance.* MIT Press.

Becker, R. (2009). *International branch campuses: Markets and strategies.* Observatory on Borderless Higher Education.

Belfield, C., & Bailey, T. (2017). *The labor market returns to sub-baccalaureate college: A review.* Center for Analysis of Postsecondary Education and Employment, Columbia University.

Bénabou, R., & Tirole, J. (2003). Intrinsic and extrinsic motivation. *Review of Economic Studies, 70*(3), 489–520.

Bennett, D. (2014). Clayton Christensen responds to *New Yorker* takedown of "disruptive innovation." *Bloomberg Business.* http://www.bloomberg.com/bw/articles/2014-06-20/clayton-christensen-responds-to-new-yorker-takedown-of-disruptive-innovation

Berkun, S. (2007). *The myths of innovation.* O'Reilly.

Bhagwati, J., Panagariya, A., & Srinivasan, R. N. (2004). The muddles over oversourcing. *Journal of Economic Perspectives, 18*(4), 93–114.

Bigley, G. A., & Pearce, I. L. (1998). Straining for shared meaning in organizational science: Problems of trust and distrust. *Academy of Management Review, 23*(3), 405–421.

Birkinshaw, J., & Hamel, G., & Mol, M. J. (2008). Management innovation. *Academy of Management Review, 33*(4), 825–845.

Bloomberg NEF (2020). Electric vehicle outlook 2020. Bloomberg NEF. https://bnef.turtl.co/story/evo-2020

Blumenstyk, G. (2018). Here's how Western Governors U. aims to enroll a million students. *Chronicle of Higher Education.* https://www.chronicle.com/article/Here-s-How-Western-Governors/243492

Bowen, W. G. (2012). The "cost disease" in higher education: Is technology the answer? Palo Alto, CA: Tanner Lecture, Stanford University. https://www.ithaka.org/sites/default/files/files/ITHAKA-TheCostDiseaseinHigherEducation.pdf

Brennan, G. (1998). Democratic trust: A rational-choice theory view. In V. Braithwaite & M. Levi (Eds.), *Trust and governance* (pp. 197–217). Russell Sage Foundation.

Brewer, D., & Tierney, W. G. (2012). Barriers to innovation in U.S. education. In B. Wildavsky, A. P. Kelly, & K. Carey (Eds.), *Reinventing higher education: The promise of innovation* (pp. 11–40). Harvard Education Press.

Breznitz, D. (2014). Why Germany dominates the U.S. in innovation. *Harvard Business Review.* https://hbr.org/2014/05/why-germany-dominates-the-u-s-in-innovation

Brown, G. (2018). Online education policy and practice: The past, present, and the future of the digital university. *American Journal of Distance Education*, *32*(2), 156–158.

Brown, K. W., & Ryan, R. M. (2003). The benefits of being present: Mindfulness and its role in psychological well-being. *Journal of Personality and Social Psychology*, *84*(4), 822–848.

Brunner, J. J. (2013). New dynamics of Latin American higher education. *International Higher Education*, *71*, 20–22.

Bruno-Jofré, R., & Schriewer, J. (Eds.). (2012). *The global reception of John Dewey's thought: Multiple refractions through time and space*. Routledge.

Brynjolfsson, E., & McAfee, A. (2011). *Race against the machine: How the digital revolution is accelerating innovation, driving productivity, and irreversibly transforming employment and the economy*. Digital Frontier Press

Buller, J. L. (2015). *Change leadership in higher education: A practical guide to academic transformation*. Jossey Bass.

Burd, S. (2017). *Moving on up?* New America.

Busta, H. (2019). How many colleges and universities have closed since 2016? *Education Dive*. https://www.educationdive.com/news/how-many-colleges-and-universities-have-closed-since-2016/539379/

California Department of Education. (2017). Research on school counseling effectiveness. https://www.cde.ca.gov/ls/cg/rh/counseffective.asp

Callan, P. (2012). The perils of success: Clark Kerr and the Californian master plan for higher education. In S. Rothblatt (Ed.), *Clark Kerr's world of higher education reaches the 21st century: Chapters in a special history* (pp. 61–84). Springer.

Campbell, J. (2020). Ex machina: Technological disruption and the future of artificial intelligence in legal writing. University of Denver Legal Studies Research Paper No. 20-4. SSRN. https://ssrn.com/abstract=3544233

Cantwell, B. (2015). Are international students cash cows? Examining the relationship between new international undergraduate enrollment and institutional revenue at public colleges and universities in the U.S. *Journal of International Students*, *5*(4), 512–525.

Carlile, P. R., & Lakhani, K. R. (2011). Innovation and the challenge of novelty: The novelty-confirmation-transformation cycle in software and science (Working Paper 11-096). Harvard Business School. http://www.hbs.edu/faculty/Publication%20Files/11-096.pdf

Carnevale, A. P., Rose, S. J., & Cheah, B. (2013). *The college payoff: Education, occupations, lifetime earnings*. Center on Education and the Workforce, Georgetown Public Policy Institute.

Carnevale, A. P., Smith, N., & Strohl, J. (2014). *Recovery: Job growth and education requirements through 2020*. Center on Education and the Workforce, Georgetown Public Policy Institute.

Carnevale, A. P., Smith, N., Melton, M., & Price, E. W. (2015). *Learning while earning: The new normal.* Center on Education and the Workforce, Georgetown University.

Castells, M. (2004). Informationalism, networks, and the network society: A theoretical blueprint. In M. Castells (Ed.), *The network society: A cross-cultural perspective* (pp. 3–45). Edward Elgar.

Cellini, S. R., & Koedel, C. (2017). The case for limiting federal student aid to for-profit colleges. *Journal of Policy Analysis and Management, 36*(4), 934–942.

Cellini, S. R., & Turner, N. (2018). Gainfully employed? Assessing the employment and earnings of for-profit college students using administrative data (NBER Working Paper No. 22287). National Bureau of Economic Research.

Chaffee, E. E., & Tierney, W. G. (1988). *Collegiate culture and leadership strategies.* MacMillan.

Chafkin, M. (2013). Udacity's Sebastian Thrun, godfather of free online education, changes course. *Fast Company.* https://www.fastcompany.com/3021473/udacity-sebastian-thrun-uphill-climb

Chan, R. Y., Bista, K., & Allen, R. M. (2021). *Online teaching and learning in higher education during covid-19: International perspectives and experiences.* Routledge.

Choudaha, R. (2017). Are international students "cash cows?" *International Higher Education, 90,* 5–6.

Christensen, C. M. (1997). *The innovator's dilemma: When new technologies cause great firms to fail.* Harvard Business School Press.

Christensen, C. M., & Eyring, H. J. (2011). *The innovative university: Changing the DNA of higher education from the inside out.* Jossey-Bass.

Christensen, C. M., Horn, M. B., Caldera, L., & Soares, L. (2011). *Disrupting college: How disruptive innovation can deliver quality and affordability to postsecondary education. Washington, DC: Center for American Progress.* https://cdn.americanprogress.org/wp-content/uploads/issues/2011/02/pdf/disrupting_college.pdf

Christensen, C. M., & Raynor, M. E. (2003). *The innovator's solution: Creating and sustaining successful growth.* Harvard Business School Press.

Christensen, C. M., & Raynor, M. E., & McDonald, R. (2015). What is disruptive innovation? *Harvard Business Review.* https://hbr.org/2015/12/what-is-disruptive-innovation

Christensen, C. M., & van Bever, D. (2014). The capitalist's dilemma. *Harvard Business Review, 92,* 60–68.

Christensen, G., Steinmetz, A., Alcorn, B., Bennett, A., Woods, D., & Emanuel, E. (2013). The MOOC phenomenon: Who takes massive open online courses and why? (Working Paper). SSRN. https://doi.org/10.2139/ssrn.2350964

Clark, B. R. (1970). *The distinctive college.* Aldine.

Clark, B. R. (1998). *Creating entrepreneurial universities: Organizational pathways of transformation.* Emerald.

Clynes, T. (2016). Peter Theil's dropout army. *New York Times*. https://www.nytimes.com/2016/06/05/opinion/sunday/peter-thiels-dropout-army.html

Comin, D. (2016). *Drivers of competitiveness*. World Scientific.

Cooper, J. R. (1998). A multidimensional approach to the adoption of innovation. *Management Decision, 36*(8), 493–502.

Cottom, T. M. (2017). *Lower ed: The troubling rise of for-profit colleges in the new economy*. The New Press.

Coupe, T. (2003). Science is golden: Academic R&D and university patents. *Journal of Technology Transfer, 28*(1), 31–46.

Craig, R. (2015). *College disrupted: The great unbundling of higher education*. St. Martin's Press.

Crane, R. (2017). *Mindfulness-based cognitive therapy*. Routledge.

Crescenzi, R., & Rodríguez-Pose, A. (2011). *Innovation and regional growth in the European Union*. Springer.

Creswell, J. D. (2017). Mindfulness interventions. *Annual Review of Psychology, 68*, 491–516.

Crossan, M. M., & Apaydin, M. (2010). A multi-dimensional framework of organizational innovation: A systematic review of the literature. *Journal of Management Studies, 47*(6), 1154–1191.

Crow, M. M., & Dabars, W. B. (2020). *The fifth wave: The evolution of American higher education*. Johns Hopkins University Press.

Daft, R. L., & Becker, S. W. (1978). *The innovative organization*. Elsevier.

Daniel, B. (2015). Big data and analytics in higher education: Opportunities and challenges. *British Journal of Educational Technology, 46*(5), 904–920.

Daniels, R. J., & Spector, P. (2016). *Converging paths: Public and private research universities in the 21st century*. TIAA Institute. https://www.tiaainstitute.org/public/pdf/converging_paths_daniels_spector.pdf

Darder, A. (2012). Neoliberalism in the academic borderlands: An ongoing struggle for equality and human rights. *Educational Studies, 48*(5), 412–426.

Das, M., & Hilgenstock, B. (2018). *The exposure to routinization: Labor market implications for developed and developing economies*. International Monetary Fund.

Das, T., & Teng, B. (2001). Trust, control, and risk in strategic alliances: An integrated framework. *Organization Studies, 22*(2), 251–283.

D'Aveni, R. A. (1994). *Hypercompetition: Managing the dynamics of strategic maneuvering*. Free Press.

de Sousa Santos, B. (2012). The university at a crossroads. *Human Architecture, 10*(1), Article 3.

Deci, E. L., Ryan, R. M., & Koestner, R. (1999). A meta-analytic review of experiments examining the effects of extrinsic rewards on intrinsic motivation. *Psychological Bulletin, 125*(6), 627–668.

Dede, C. J., Ho, A. D., & Mitros, P. (2016). Big data analysis in higher education: Promises and pitfalls. *EDUCAUSE Review, 51*(5). https://er.educause.edu/articles/2016/8/big-data-analysis-in-higher-education-promises-and-pitfalls

Deem, R., & Brehony, K. J. (2005). Management as ideology: The case of "new managerialism" in higher education. *Oxford Review of Education, 31*(2), 217–235.

Deming, D. J., Goldin, C., Katz, L. F., & Yuchtman, N. (2015). Can online learning bend the higher education cost curve? (NBER Working Paper 20890). National Bureau of Economic Research. https://www.nber.org/papers/w20890

Dent, M., & Barry, J. (2017). New public management and the professions in the U.K.: Reconfiguring control? In M. Dent, J. Chandler, & J. Barry (Eds.), *Questioning the new public management* (2nd ed.) (pp. 7–22). Routledge.

Dess, G. G., & Picken, J. C. (2000). Changing roles: Leadership in the 21st century. *Organizational Dynamics, 28*(3), 18–34.

Dodgson, M., & Gann, D. (2010). *Innovation: A very short introduction.* New York: Oxford University Press.

Dougherty, K. J., Lahr, H., & Morest, V. S. (2017). *Reforming the American community college: Promising changes and their challenges.* Community College Research Center, Columbia University.

Drucker, P. F. (2014). *Innovation and entrepreneurship.* Routledge.

Dunbar, J., & Donald, D. (2009). *The roots of the financial crisis: Who is to blame?* Center for Public Integrity. https://publicintegrity.org/business/the-roots-of-the-financial-crisis-who-is-to-blame/

Edelstein, R. J., & Douglass, J. A. (2012). *Comprehending the international initiatives of universities: A taxonomy of modes of engagement and institutional logics* (Research and occasional paper series 19.12). Center for Studies in Higher Education, University of California, Berkeley.

Eisenhardt, K. M., & Tabrizi, B. N. (1995). Accelerating adaptive processes: Product innovation in the global computer industry. *Administrative Science Quarterly, 40*(1), 84–100.

Elangovan, A., & Shapiro, D. (1998). Betrayal of trust in organizations. *Academy of Management Review, 23*(3), 547–566.

Erickson, M., Hanna, P., & Walker, C. (2021). The U.K. higher education senior management survey: A statactivist response to managerialist governance. *Studies in Higher Education, 46*(11), 2134–2151.

Estermann, T., Pruvot, E. B., Kupriyanova, V., & Stoyanova, H. (2020). *The impact of the Covid-19 crisis on university funding in Europe.* European University Association.

Erwin, D. H., & Krakauer, D. C. (2004). Insights into innovation. *Science, 304,* 1117–1119.

Ezell, S. (2019). *The Bayh-Dole Act's vital importance to the U.S. life-sciences innovation system.* Information Technology and Innovation Foundation. https://itif.org/publications/2019/03/04/bayh-dole-acts-vital-importance-us-life-sciences-innovation-system

Fagerberg, J., Fosaas, M., & Sapprasert, K. (2012). Innovation: Exploring the knowledge base. *Research Policy, 41,* 1132–1153.

Fagerberg, J., & Verspagen, B. (2009). Innovation studies—The emerging structure of a new scientific field. *Research Policy, 38*, 218–233.

Fastabend, D. A., & Simpson, R. H. (2004). *"Adapt or die": The imperative for a culture of innovation in the United States Army.* http://www.au.af.mil/au/awc/awcgate/army/culture_of_innovation.pdf

Feldman, M. P. (2002). The internet revolution and the geography of innovation. *International Social Science Journal, 54*, 47–56.

Ferreira, J. J., Fayolle, A., Ratten, V., & Raposo, M. (Eds.). (2018). *Entrepreneurial universities: Collaboration, education, and policies.* Elgar.

Finney, J. E., Riso, C., Orosz, K., & Boland, W. C. (2014). *From master plan to mediocrity: Higher education performance and policy in California.* Institute for Research on Higher Education, University of Pennsylvania.

Fisher, C. D. (1978). The effects of personal control, competence, and extrinsic reward systems on intrinsic motivation. *Organizational Behavior and Human Performance, 21*(3), 273–288.

Florida, R. (2013). The learning region. In Z. J. Acs (Ed.), *Regional innovation, knowledge, and global change* (pp. 231–239). Routledge.

Florida, R., Gates, G., Knudsen, B., & Stolarick, K. (2006). *The university and the creative economy.* http://creativeclass.com/rfcgdb/articles/University_andthe_Creative_Economy.pdf

Fong, T. T. (2006). The effects of emotional ambiguity on creativity. *Academy of Management Journal, 49*, 1016–1030.

Forster, J., Friedman, R. S., & Liberman, N. (2004). Temporal construal effects on abstract and concrete thinking: Consequences for insight and creative cognition. *Journal of Personality and Social Psychology, 87*, 177–189.

Foss, L., & Gibson, D. V. (Eds.). (2015). *The entrepreneurial university: Context and institutional change.* Routledge.

Frame, W. S., & White, L. J. (2014). *Technological change, financial innovation, and diffusion in banking* (NYU Working Paper No. 2451/33549). New York University.

Free-for-all: Open-access scientific publishing is gaining ground. (2013). *The Economist.* http://www.economist.com/news/science-and-technology/21577035-open-access-scientific-publishing-gaining-ground-free-all

Friedman, R. S., & Forster, J. (2001). The effects of promotion and prevention cues on creativity. *Journal of Personality and Social Psychology, 81*, 1001–1013.

Friedman, T. (2013). Revolution hits the universities. *New York Times.* https://www.nytimes.com/2013/01/27/opinion/sunday/friedman-revolution-hits-the-universities.html

Friga, P. N. (2021). How much has Covid cost colleges? $183 billion. *Chronicle of Higher Education.* https://www.chronicle.com/article/how-to-fight-covids-financial-crush

Frey, C. B., & Osborne, M. A. (2017). The future of employment: How suscepti-ble are jobs to computerization? *Technological Forecasting and Social Change*, *114*, 254–280.

Fry, R. (2014). *The growth in student debt*. Washington, DC: Pew Research Center. http://www.pewsocialtrends.org/2014/10/07/the-growth-in-student-debt

Galanakis, K. (2006). Innovation process: Make sense using systems thinking. *Technovation, 26*(11), 1222–1232.

Garrett, R. (2002). *International branch campuses: Scale and significance*. Observatory on Borderless Higher Education.

Gelles, D. (2019). Why "mindfulness" is at risk of becoming another buzzword. *Mindbodygreen*. https://www.mindbodygreen.com/0-17107/why-mindfulness-is-at-risk-of-becoming-just-another-buzzword.html

Gerber, L. G. (2014). *The rise and decline of faculty governance: Professionalization and the modern American university*. Johns Hopkins University Press.

Gertner, J. (2012). *The idea factory: Bell labs and the great age of American innova-tion*. Penguin Books.

Gibb, A., Haskins, G., & Robertson, I. (2013). Leading the entrepreneurial uni-versity: Meeting the entrepreneurial development needs of higher education institution. In A. Altmann & B. Ebersberger (Eds.), *Universities in change: Innovation, technology, and knowledge management* (pp. 9–45). Springer.

Gilbert, C. (2014). What Jill Lepore gets wrong about Clayton Christensen and dis-ruptive innovation. *Forbes*. http://www.forbes.com/sites/forbesleadershipforum/2014/06/30/what-jill-lepore-gets-wrong-about-clayton-christensen-and-disruptive-innovation/#706a01e71ccc

Gillespie, N., & Dietz, G. (2009). Trust repair after an organization-level failure. *Academy of Management Review, 34*(1), 127–145.

Giroux, H. (2015). Higher education and the politics of disruption. *Truthout*. https://truthout.org/articles/higher-education-and-the-politics-of-disruption/

Goddard, B. (2012). *Future perspectives: Horizon 2025. In D. V. Davis & B. Mack-intosh (Eds.), Making a difference: Australian international education*. University of New South Wales Press.

Godin, B. (2006). The linear model of innovation: The historical construction of an analytical framework. *Science, Technology, and Human Values, 31*(6), 639–667.

Godin, B. (2008). In the shadow of Schumpeter: W. Rupert Maclaurin and the study of technological innovation. *Project on the Intellectual History of Innovation, 2*, Montreal: INRS. http://www.csiic.ca/pdf/intellectualno2.pdf

Godin, B. (2014). The vocabulary of innovation: A lexicon. *Project on the Intellectual History of Innovation, 20*, Montreal: INRS. Paper presented at the 2nd CASTI Workshop, Agder, Norway. http://www.csiic.ca/PDF/LexiconPaperNo20.pdf

Goethe Institute. (2015). *Land of inventors*. http://www.goethe.de/lhr/prj/ede/suf/enindex.htm

Goffman, E. (1961/1977). The characteristics of total institutions. In C. Lemert & A. Branaman (Eds.)., *The Goffman reader* (pp. 55–63). Blackwell.

Goldrick-Rab, S. (2016). *Paying the price.* University of Chicago Press.

Gonzales, L. D., Hall, K., Benton, A., Kanhai, D., & Núñez, A. (2021). Comfort over change: A case study of diversity and inclusivity efforts in U.S. higher education. *Innovative Higher Education, 46*(5), 445–460.

Gonzales, L. D., Martinez, E., & Ordu, C. (2014). Exploring faculty experiences in a striving university through the lens of academic capitalism. *Studies in Higher Education, 39*(7), 1097–1115.

Gould, E. (2017). *The state of American wages 2016.* Economic Policy Institute. https://www.epi.org/publication/the-state-of-american-wages-2016-lower-unemployment-finally-helps-working-people-make-up-some-lost-ground-on-wages/

Grawe, N. (2018). *Demographics and the demand for higher education.* Johns Hopkins University Press.

Grawe, N. (2021). *The agile college: How institutions successfully navigate demographic changes.* Johns Hopkins University Press.

Gulley, N. (2016). The myth of the non-traditional student. *Inside Higher Ed.* https://www.insidehighered.com/views/2016/08/05/defining-students-nontraditional-inaccurate-and-damaging-essay

Gut, A., Wilczewski, M., & Gorbaniuk, O. (2017). Cultural differences, stereotypes, and communication needs in intercultural communication in a global multicultural environment: The employees' perspective. *Journal of Intercultural Communication, 43.* http://www.immi.se/intercultural/nr43/gorbaniuk.html

Hackman, M., & Belkin, D. (2018). Fewer international students heading to the U.S. *Wall Street Journal.* https://www.wsj.com/articles/fewer-international-students-heading-to-the-u-s-1542105004

Hamer, J. F., & Lang, C. (2015). Race, structural violence, and the neoliberal university: The challenges of inhabitation. *Critical Sociology, 41*(6), 897–912.

Hannon, P. D. (2013). Why is the entrepreneurial university important? *Journal of Innovation Management, 1*(2).

Harmon, O., Hopkins, B., Kelchen, R., Persky, J., & Roy, J. (2018). The annual report on the economic status of the profession, 2017–18. *Academe, 104*(2), 4–10.

Harper, S. (2020). Covid-19 and the racial equity implications of reopening college and university campuses. *American Journal of Education, 127*(1), 153–162.

Hasanefendic, S., Birkholz, J. M., Horta, H., & van der Sijde, P. (2017). Individuals in action: Bringing about innovation in higher education. *European Journal of Higher Education, 7*(2), 101–119.

Hathaway, R. L. (1995). *Not necessarily Cervantes: Readings of the "Quixote."* Juan de la Cuesta.

Hazboun, S. O., & Boudet, H. S. (2020). Public preferences in a shifting energy future: Comparing public views of eight energy sources in North America's Pacific Northwest. *Energies, 13*(8), 1940.

Hemel, D., & Ouellette, L. L. (2017). Bayh-Dole beyond borders. Chicago Unbound, Coase-Sandor Working Paper Series in Law and Economics. https://chicago unbound.uchicago.edu/cgi/viewcontent.cgi?article=2490&context=law_and_ economics

Henderson, R., Jaffe, A., & Trajtenberg, M. (1998). Universities as a source of commercial technology: A detailed analysis of university patenting: 1965–1988. *Review of Economics and Statistics, 80*(1), 119–127.

Hess, A. (2018). Harvard business school professor: Half of American colleges will be bankrupt in 10 to 15 years. *CNBC.com*. https://www.cnbc.com/2018/08/30/ hbs-prof-says-half-of-us-colleges-will-be-bankrupt-in-10-to-15-years.html

Hewlett, S. A., Marshall, M., & Sherbin, L. (2013). How diversity can drive innovation. *Harvard Business Review*. https://hbr.org/2013/12/how-diversity-can-drive-innovation

Hill, P., & Roza, M. (2010). Curing Baumol's disease: In search of productivity gains in k-12 schooling (CRPE White Paper 2010_1) [White paper]. Center on Reinventing Public Education, University of Washington at Bothell. https:// edunomicslab.org/wp-content/uploads/2013/12/whp_crpe1_baumols_jul10_0. pdf

Hillman, N. W., Tandberg, D. A., & Fryar, A. H. (2015). Evaluating the impacts of "new" performance funding in higher education. *Educational Evaluation and Policy Analysis, 37*(4), 501–519.

Hiltzik, M. A. (1999). *Dealers of lightning: Xerox parc and the dawn of the computer age*. Harper.

Himmelstein, J. L., & Zald, M. (1984). American conservatism and government funding of the social sciences and the arts. *Sociological Inquiry, 54*(2), 171–187.

Hirsch, F. (1976). *Social limits to growth*. Routledge.

Hixon, T. (2014). Higher education is now ground zero for disruption. *Forbes*. http:// www.forbes.com/sites/toddhixon/2014/01/06/higher-education-is-now-ground-zero-for-disruption/#4c95283c5bd9

Hoecht, A., & Trott, P. (2006). Innovation risks of strategic outsourcing. *Technovation, 26*(5–6), 672–681.

Hollander, J. E., & Carr, B. G. (2020). Virtually perfect? Telemedicine for Covid-19. *New England Journal of Medicine 382*(18), 1679–1681.

Hood, C. (1995). The "new public management" in the 1980s: Variations on a theme. *Accounting, Organizations, and Society, 20*(2/3), 93–109.

Horn, M. (2018). Will half of all colleges really close in the next decade? *Forbes*. https://www.forbes.com/sites/michaelhorn/2018/12/13/will-half-of-all-colleges-really-close-in-the-next-decade

Horn, M. (2019). How Harvard hurts small colleges. *Education Next.* https://www.educationnext.org/harvard-hurts-small-colleges

Howe, J. (2013, February 12). Clayton Christensen wants to transform capitalism. *Wired.* https://www.wired.com/2013/02/mf-clayton-christensen-wants-to-transform-capitalism

Hunt, V., Layton, D., & Prince, S. (2014). *Diversity matters.* McKinsey & Company. http://www.mckinsey.com/~/media/McKinsey%20Offices/United%20Kingdom/PDFs/Diversity_matters_2014.ashx

International Energy Agency. (2020). *Innovation in batteries and electricity storage: A global analysis based on patent data.* International Energy Agency. https://www.iea.org/reports/innovation-in-batteries-and-electricity-storage

Jackson, V., & Saenz, M. (2021). *States can choose better path for higher education funding in Covid-19 recession.* Center on Budget and Policy Priorities.

Janeway, W. H. (2012). *Doing capitalism in the innovation economy: Markets, speculation, and the state.* Cambridge University Press.

Jaschik, S. (2018). Falling confidence in higher ed. *Inside Higher Ed.* https://www.insidehighered.com/news/2018/10/09/gallup-survey-finds-falling-confidence-higher-education

Jaschik, S. (2019, March 18). The week that shook college admissions. *Inside Higher Ed.* https://www.insidehighered.com/admissions/article/2019/03/18/look-how-indictments-shook-college-admissions

Johnson, S. (2018). Are you still there? How a "Netflix" model for advising lost its luster. *EdSurge.* https://www.edsurge.com/news/2018-03-15-are-you-still-there-how-a-netflix-model-for-advising-lost-its-luster

Johnson, H., Mejia, M. C., & Bohn, S. (2015). *Will California run out of college graduates?* Public Policy Institute of California.

Jongbloed, B., Enders, J., & Salerno, C. (2008). Higher education and its communities: Interconnections, interdependencies, and a research agenda. *Higher Education, 56,* 303–324.

Jubas, K. (2012). On being a new academic in the new academy: Impacts of neoliberalism on work and life of a junior faculty member. *Workplace: A Journal for Academic Labor, 21,* n.p.

Kabat-Zinn, J. (1994). *Wherever you go, there you are: Mindfulness meditation in everyday life.* Hyperion.

Kabat-Zinn, J. (2003). Mindfulness-based interventions in context: Past, present, and future. *Clinical Psychology: Science and Practice, 10*(2), 144–156.

Kalamkarian, H. S., Karp, M. M., & Ganga, E. (2017a). *Advising redesign as a foundation for transformative change.* Community College Research Center, Columbia University.

Kalamkarian, H. S., Karp, M. M., & Ganga, E. (2017b). *Creating the conditions for advising redesign.* Community College Research Center, Columbia University.

Kalamkarian, H. S., Karp, M. M., & Ganga, E. (2017c). *What we know about technology-mediated advising reform*. Community College Research Center, Columbia University.

Kanarfogel, D. A. (2009). Rectifying the missing costs of university patent practices: Addressing Bayh-Dole criticisms through faculty involvement. *Cardozo Arts and Entertainment Law Journal, 27*(2), 533–544.

Kelchen, R. (2017). *How much do for-profit colleges rely on federal funds?* Washington, DC: Brookings Institution. https://www.brookings.edu/blog/brown-center-chalkboard/2017/01/11/how-much-do-for-profit-colleges-rely-on-federal-funds/

Kenney, M., & Patton, D. (2009). Reconsidering the Bayh-Dole Act and the current university invention ownership model. *Research Policy, 38*, 1407–1422.

Keyishian v. Board of Regents of Univ. of State of N.Y. (1967). *Oyez*. https://www.oyez.org/cases/1966/105

Kezar, A. (2004). Obtaining integrity? Reviewing and examining the charter between higher education and society. *Review of Higher Education, 27*(4), 429–459.

Kezar, A., & Maxey, D. (2013). The changing academic workforce. *Trusteeship, 21*(3), 15–21.

Khavul, S., & Bruton, G. D. (2012). Harnessing innovation for change: Sustainability and poverty in developing countries. *Journal of Management Studies, 50*(2), 285–306.

Kim, J., & Maloney, E. (2020). *Learning innovation and the future of higher education*. Johns Hopkins University Press.

Kimball, B. A., & Johnson, B. A. (2012). The beginning of 'free money' ideology in American universities: Charles W. Eliot at Harvard, 1869–1909. *History of Education Quarterly, 52*(2), 222–250.

King, A. A., & Baatartogtokh, B. (2015). How useful is the theory of disruptive innovation? *MIT Sloan Management Review*, 77–90.

Kline, S. J., & Rosenberg, N. (1986). An overview of innovation. In R. Landau & N. Rosenberg (Eds.), *The positive sum strategy: Harnessing technology for economic growth* (pp. 275–305). National Academy Press.

Knight, J. (2011). Education hubs: A fad, a brand, an innovation? *Journal of Studies in International Education, 15*(3), 221–240.

Knight, J., & Morshidi, S. (2011). The complexities and challenges of regional education hubs: Focus on Malaysia. *Higher Education, 62*(5), 593–606.

Knight, J. (2018). International education hubs. In P. Meusburger, M. Heffernan, & L. Suarsana (Eds.), *Geographies of the university* (pp. 637–655). Springer.

Konnikova, M. (2014). Will MOOCs be flukes? *New Yorker*. https://www.newyorker.com/science/maria-konnikova/moocs-failure-solutions

Koselleck, R. (1972). Begriffsgeschichte and social history. In R. Koselleck (Ed.), *Futures past: On the semantics of historical time* (pp. 75–92), Columbia University Press.

Kretovics, M. (2018). Education or revenue generation? Revisiting business practices in higher education. *The Evolllution.* https://evolllution.com/managing-institution/higher_ed_business/education-or-revenue-generation-revisiting-business-practices-in-higher-education

Krupnick, M., & Marcus, J. (2015). Think university administrators' salaries are high? Critics say their benefits are lavish. *Hechinger Report.* https://hechinger-report.org/think-university-administrators-salaries-are-high-critics-say-their-benefits-are-lavish/

Ladegaard, H. J., & Jenks, C. J. (2015). Language and intercultural communication in the workplace: Critical approaches to theory and practice. *Language and Intercultural Communication, 15*(1), 1–12.

Lam, T. W., & Chiu, C-Y. (2002). The motivational function of regulatory focus in creativity. *Journal of Creative Behavior, 36*, 138–150.

Lane, J. E. (2014). *Building a smarter university: Big data, innovation, and analytics.* SUNY Press.

Lanford, M. (2016). Perceptions of higher education reform in Hong Kong: A glocalization perspective. *International Journal of Comparative Education and Development, 18*(3), 183–204.

Lanford, M. (2020). Long term sustainability in global higher education partnerships. In A. Al-Youbi, A. Zahed, & W. G. Tierney (Eds.), Successful global collaborations in higher education institutions (pp. 87–93). Springer.

Lanford, M. (2021). Institutional competition through performance funding: A catalyst or hindrance to teaching and learning? *Educational Philosophy and Theory, 53*(1), 1148–1160.

Lanford, M., Corwin, Z. B., Maruco, T., & Ochsner, A. (2019). Institutional barriers to innovation: Lessons from a digital intervention to improve college access for low-income students. *Journal of Research on Technology in Education, 51*(3), 203–216.

Lanford, M., & Maruco, T. (2018). When job training is not enough: The cultivation of social capital in career academies. *American Educational Research Journal, 55*(3), 617–648.

Lanford, M., & Maruco, T. (2019). Six conditions for successful career academies. *Phi Delta Kappan, 100*(5), 50–52.

Lanford, M., & Tierney, W. G. (2015). *From "vocational education" to "linked learning": The ongoing transformation of career-oriented education in the United States.* Los Angeles, CA: Pullias Center for Higher Education, University of Southern California. https://files.eric.ed.gov/fulltext/ED574633.pdf

Lanford, M., & Tierney, W. G. (2016). The international branch campus: Cloistered community or agent of social change? In D. Neubauer, J. Hawkins, M. Lee, & C. Collins (Eds.), *The Palgrave handbook of Asia Pacific higher education* (pp. 157–172). Palgrave Macmillan.

Lanford, M., & Tierney, W. G. (2018). Re-envisioning graduate and early career socialization to encourage public scholarship. In A. Kezar, Y. Drivalas, &

J. A. Kitchen (Eds.), *Envisioning public scholarship for our time: Models for higher education researchers* (pp. 163–178). Stylus.

Langfred, C. W. (2004). Too much of a good thing? Negative effects of high trust and individual autonomy in self-managing teams. *Academy of Management Journal, 47*(3), 385–399.

Lauder, H., & Mayhew, K. (2020). Higher education and the labour market: An introduction. *Oxford Review of Education, 46*(1), 1–9.

Lawless, B., & Chen, Y.-W. (2017). Multicultural neoliberalism and academic labor: Experiences of female immigrant faculty in the U.S. academy. *Cultural Studies <-> Critical Methodologies, 17*(3), 236–243.

Leary, J. P. (2018). Enough will all the innovation. *Chronicle of Higher Education.* https://www.chronicle.com/article/Enough-With-All-the-Innovation/245044

Lederman, D. (2017). Clay Christensen, doubling down. *Inside Higher Ed.* https://www.insidehighered.com/digital-learning/article/2017/04/28/clay-christensen-sticks-predictions-massive-college-closures

Lederman, D. (2018a). A quarter of private colleges ran deficits in 2017. *Inside Higher Ed.* https://www.insidehighered.com/quicktakes/2018/06/27/quarter-private-colleges-ran-deficits-2017

Lederman, D. (2018b). Online education ascends. *Inside Higher Ed.* https://www.insidehighered.com/digital-learning/article/2018/11/07/new-data-online-enrollments-grow-and-share-overall-enrollment

Leiber, N. (2019). Foreign students sour on America, jeopardizing a $39 billion industry. *Bloomberg.* https://www.bloomberg.com/news/articles/2019-01-17/foreign-students-are-a-39-billion-industry-trump-is-scaring-them-off

Lenzner, R., & Johnson, S. S. (1997). Seeing things as they really are. *Forbes.* https://www.forbes.com/forbes/1997/0310/5905122a.html#5ba44fd24b9f

Lepore, J. (2014). The disruption machine. *The New Yorker.* http://www.newyorker.com/magazine/2014/06/23/the-disruption-machine

Leung, A. K., Maddux, W. W., Galinsky, A. D., & Chiu, C. (2008). Multicultural experience enhances creativity: The when and how. *American Psychologist, 63*(3), 169–181.

Levin, J. S., & Aliyeva, A. (2015). Embedded neoliberalism within faculty behaviors. *Review of Higher Education, 38*(4), 537–563.

Levine, L. H. (2011). *Offshoring (or offshore outsourcing) and job loss among U.S. workers.* Congressional Research Service Report 7–5700. U.S. Congressional Research Service.

Liao, F., Molin, E., & van Wee, B. (2017). Consumer preferences for electric vehicles: A literature review. *Transport Reviews, 37*(3), 252–275.

Liera, R. (2020). Moving beyond a culture of niceness in faculty hiring to advance racial equity. *American Educational Research Journal, 57*(5), 1954–1994.

Lightcap, T.L.R. (2014). Academic governance and democratic processes: The entrepreneurial model and its discontents. *New Political Science, 36*(4), 474–488.

Littlejohn, A., & Hood, N. (2018). *Reconceptualizing learning in the digital age: The [un]democratizing potential of MOOCs.* Springer.

Lorenz, C. (2012). If you're so smart, why are you under surveillance? Universities, neoliberalism, and new public management. *Critical Inquiry, 38*(3), 599–629.

Low, M. B., & MacMillan, I. C. (1988). Entrepreneurship: Past research and future challenges. *Journal of Management, 14*(2), 139–161.

Lumina Foundation. (n.d.). Goal 2025. http://strategylabs.luminafoundation.org/goal-2025/

Lynch, K. (2015). Control by numbers: New managerialism and ranking in higher education. *Critical Studies in Education, 56*(2), 190–207.

Maldonado, C. (2018). Price of college increasing almost eight time faster than wages. *Forbes.* https://www.forbes.com/sites/camilomaldonado/2018/07/24/price-of-college-increasing-almost-8-times-faster-than-wages/#70a9d88266c1

Manyika, J., Chui, M., Bughin, J., Dobbs, R., Bisson, P., & Marra, A. (2013). *Disruptive technologies: Advances that will transform life, business, and the global economy.* McKinsey Global Institute. http://www.mckinsey.com/insights/business_technology/disruptive_technologies

Manyika, J., Chui, M., Miremadi, M., Bughin, J., George, K., Wilmott, P., Dewhurst, M. (2017a). *A future that works: Automation, employment, and productivity.* McKinsey Global Institute.

Manyika, J., Lund, S., Bughin, J., Woetzel, J., Stamenov, K., & Dhingra, D. (2016). *Digital globalization: The new era of global flows.* McKinsey Global Institute.

Manyika, J., Lund, S., Chui, M., Bughin, J., Woetzel, J., Batra, P., Ko, R., & Sanghvi, S. (2017b). *Jobs lost, jobs gained: What the future of work will mean for jobs, skills, and wages.* McKinsey Global Institute.

Marcus, J. (2017a). Graduate programs have become a cash cow for struggling colleges. What does that mean for students? *PBS Newshour.* https://www.pbs.org/newshour/education/graduate-programs-become-cash-cow-struggling-colleges-mean-students

Marcus, J. (2017b). Universities and colleges struggle to stem big drops in enrollment. *Hechinger Report.* https://hechingerreport.org/universities-colleges-struggle-stem-big-drops-enrollment

Marcus, J. (2021). More colleges and universities outsource services to for-profit companies. *Hechinger Report.* https://hechingerreport.org/more-colleges-and-universities-outsource-services-to-for-profit-companies

Marginson, S. (2004). Competition and markets in higher education: A "glonacal" analysis. *Policy Futures in Education, 2*(2), 175–244.

Marginson, S. (2013). Labor's failure to ground public funding. In S. Marginson (Ed.), *Tertiary education policy in Australia* (pp. 59–71). Centre for the Study of Higher Education, University of Melbourne.

Marginson, S. (2016a). *The dream is over: The crisis of Clark Kerr's California idea of higher education.* University of California Press.

Marginson, S. (2016b). The worldwide trend to high participation higher education: Dynamics of social stratification in inclusive systems. *Higher Education, 72*(4), 413–434.

Marques, G., Agarwal, D., de la Torre Díez, I. (2020). Automated medical diagnosis of COVID-19 through efficient net convolutional neural network. *Applied Soft Computing, 96*, 106691.

Mars, M. M., & Rios-Aguilar, C. (2010). Academic entrepreneurship (re)defined: Significance and implications for the scholarship of higher education. *Higher Education, 59*(4), 441–460.

Mayer, C. J., & Pence, K. (2008). Subprime mortgages: What, where, and to whom? (NBER Working Paper No. 14083). National Bureau of Economic Research.

Mazzone, E. (2013). The innovation imperative: Adapt or die? *Law Practice, 39*(4), n.p. http://www.americanbar.org/publications/law_practice_magazine/2013/july-august/web-2-0.html

Mazzucato, M. (2013). *The entrepreneurial state: Debunking public vs. private sector myths.* Anthem.

McCluskey, F. B., & Winter, M. L. (2012). *The idea of the digital university: Ancient traditions, disruptive technologies, and the battle for the soul of higher education.* Washington, DC: Westphalia Press.

McLean, L. D. (2005). Organizational culture's influence on creativity and innovation: A review of the literature and implications for human resource development *Advances in Developing Human Resources, 7*, 226–246.

Meckling, J., & Hughes, L. (2018). Protecting solar: Global supply chains and business power. *New Political Economy, 23*(1), 88–104.

Medina, J., Benner, K., & Taylor, K. (2019, March 12). Actresses, business leaders, and other wealthy parents charged in U.S. college entry fraud. *New York Times.* https://www.nytimes.com/2019/03/12/us/college-admissions-cheating-scandal.html

Mehta, K., & Harles, R. (2017). In the knowledge economy, we need a netflix of education. *TechCrunch.* https://techcrunch.com/2017/07/04/in-the-knowledge-economy-we-need-a-netflix-of-education/

Meissner, D., Erdil, E., & Chataway, J. (Eds.). (2018). *Innovation and the entrepreneurial university.* Springer.

Merchant, B. (2017). *The one device: The secret history of the iPhone.* Little, Brown, and Company.

Mitchell, M., Leachman, M., & Masterson, K. (2017). *A lost decade in higher education funding.* Center on Budget and Policy Priorities.

Mitchell, M., Leachman, M., Masterson, K., & Waxman, S. (2018). *Unkept promises: State cuts to higher education threaten access and equity.* Center on Budget and Policy Priorities.

Molina-Morales, F. X., Martínez-Fernández, M. T., & Torló, V. J. (2011). The dark side of trust: The benefits, costs, and optimal levels of trust for innovation performance. *Long Range Planning, 44*(2), 118–133.

Motlteni, M. (2020). Covid-19 makes the case for more meatpacking robots. *Wired.* https://www.wired.com/story/covid-19-makes-the-case-for-more-meatpacking-robots

Murdock, T. B., & Anderman, E. M. (2006) Motivational perspective on student cheating: Toward an integrated model of academic dishonesty. *Educational Psychologist, 41*(3), 129–145.

Muscio, A., Quaglione, D., & Vallanti, G. (2013). Does government funding complement or substitute private research funding to universities? *Research Policy, 42*(1), 63–75.

Nakamura, H., & Kajikawa, Y. (2018). Regulation and innovation: How should small unmanned aerial vehicles be regulated? *Technological Forecasting and Social Change, 128,* 262–274.

Naidoo, R., & Williams, J. (2015). The neoliberal regime in English higher education: Charters, consumers, and the erosion of the public good. *Critical Studies in Education, 56*(2), 208–223.

National Association of College and University Business Officers (NACUBO). (2018). *2017 tuition discounting study.* NACUBO.

National Center for Education Statistics (NCES). (2017a). *Degree-granting postsecondary institutions, by control and level of institution: Selected years, 1949–50 through 2019–20.* Washington, DC: U.S. Department of Education. https://nces.ed.gov/programs/digest/d19/tables/dt19_317.10.asp

National Center for Education Statistics (NCES). (2017b). *Total fall enrollment in degree-granting postsecondary institutions, by attendance status, sex of student, and control of institution: Selected years, 1947 through 2029.* Washington, DC: U.S. Department of Education. https://nces.ed.gov/programs/digest/d19/tables/dt19_303.10.asp

National Science Board. (2008). *Science and engineering indicators 2008.* National Science Foundation.

Natow, R. S. (2021). Why haven't more colleges closed? *Chronicle of Higher Education.* https://www.chronicle.com/article/why-havent-more-colleges-closed

Ness, R. B. (2015). *The creativity crisis: Reinventing science to unleash possibility.* Oxford University Press.

Newton, D. (2018). Why college tuition is actually higher for online programs. *Forbes.* https://www.forbes.com/sites/dereknewton/2018/06/25/why-college-tuition-is-actually-higher-for-online-programs

Ohanian, H. C. (2008). *Einstein's mistakes: The human failings of genius.* Norton.

Okhuysen, G. A., Galinsky, A. D., & Uptigrove, T. A. (2003). Saving the worst for last: The effect of time horizon on the efficiency of negotiating benefits and burdens. *Organizational Behavior and Human Decision Processes, 91,* 269–279.

Olds, K. (2007). Global assemblage: Singapore, foreign universities, and the construction of a "global education hub." *World Development, 35*(6), 959–975.

Oleksiyenko, A. (2018). Zones of alienation in global higher education: Corporate abuse and leadership failures. *Tertiary Education and Management, 24*(3), 193–205.

Oleksiyenko, A, & Tierney, W. G. (2018). Higher education and human vulnerability: Global failures of corporate design. *Tertiary Education and Management, 24*(3), 187–192.

Oliff, P., Palacios, V., Johnson, I., & Leachman, M. (2013, March 19). *Recent deep state higher education cuts may harm students and the economy for years to come.* Center on Budget and Policy Priorities. http://www.cbpp.org/research/recent-deep-state-higher-education-cuts-may-harm-students-and-the-economy-for-years-to-come

Olssen, M. (2016). Neoliberal competition in higher education today: Research, accountability, and impact. *British Journal of Sociology of Education, 37*(1), 129–148.

Orton, J. D., & Weick, K. E. (1990). Loosely coupled systems: A reconceptualization. *Academy of Management Review, 15*(2), 203–223.

Osei-Kofi, N. (2012). Junior faculty of color in the corporate university: Implications of neoliberalism and neoconservatism on research, teaching, and service. *Critical Studies in Education, 53*(2), 229–244.

Owen, R., Bessant, J., & Heintz, M. (2013). *Responsible innovation: Managing the responsible emergence of science and innovation in society.* Wiley.

Page, T. (2014). Notions of innovation in healthcare services and products. *International Journal of Innovation and Sustainable Development, 8*(3), 217–231.

Page, L. C., & Gehlbach, H. (2017). How an artificially intelligent virtual assistant helps students navigate the road to college. *AERA Open, 3*(4). https://doi.org/10.1177/2332858417749220

Park, S. H., & Han, K. (2018). Methodologic guide for evaluating clinical performance and effect of artificial intelligence technology for medical diagnosis and prediction. *Radiology, 286*(3), 800–809.

Parthenon. (2016). *Strength in numbers: Strategies for collaborating in a new era for higher education.* Ernst & Young.

Perkins, J. F., & Tierney W. G. (2014). The Bayh-Dole Act, technology transfer, and the public interest. *Industry and Higher Education, 28*(2), 143–151.

Perna, L., Ruby, A., Boruch, R., Wang, N., Scull, J., Evans, C., & Ahmad, S. (2013). The life cycle of a million MOOC users. University of Pennsylvania. Presentation for the MOOC Research Initiative Conference. https://www.gse.upenn.edu/pdf/ahead/perna_ruby_boruch_moocs_dec2013.pdf

Petit, N. (2018). Artificial intelligence and automated law enforcement: A review paper. SSRN. https://ssrn.com/abstract=3145133

Phillips, M., & Russell, K. (2018). The next financial calamity is coming. Here's what to watch. *New York Times.* https://www.nytimes.com/interactive/2018/09/12/business/the-next-recession-financial-crisis.html

Popper, K. (1963). *Conjectures and refutations: The growth of scientific knowledge.* New York: Routledge.

Postiglione, G. (2011). Global recession and higher education in eastern Asia: China, Mongolia, and Vietnam. *Higher Education, 62*(6), 789–814.

Powell, B. A., Gilleland, D. S., & Pearson, L. C. (2012). Expenditures, efficiency, and effectiveness in U.S. undergraduate higher education: A national benchmark model. *Journal of Higher Education, 83*(1), 102–127.

Powell, W. W., Koput, K. W., & Smith-Doerr, L. (1996). Interorganizational collaboration and the locus of innovation: Networks of learning in biotechnology. *Administrative Science Quarterly, 41*(1), 116–145.

Powers, J. B. (2003). Commercializing academic research: Resource effects on performance of university technology transfer. *Journal of Higher Education, 74*(1), 26–50.

Prahalad, C. K., & Hamel, G. (1990). The core competence of the corporation. *Harvard Business Review.* https://hbr.org/1990/05/the-core-competence-of-the-corporation

Pusser, B., & Marginson, S. (2013). University rankings in critical perspective. *Journal of Higher Education, 84*(4), 544–568.

Quinn, J. B., & Hilmer, F. G. (1994). Strategic outsourcing. *Sloan Management Review, 35*(4), 43–55.

Rabitschek, J. H., & Latker, N. J. (2005). Reasonable pricing—A New twist for march-in rights under the Bayh-Dole Act. *Santa Clara High Technology Law Journal, 22*(1), art. 4.

Rademacher, T. (2020). Artificial intelligence and law enforcement. In T. Wischmeyer & T. Rademacher (Eds.), *Regulating artificial intelligence* (pp. 225–254). Springer.

Rutherford, A., & Rabovsky, T. (2014). Evaluating impacts of performance funding policies on student outcomes in higher education. *The Annals of the American Academy of Political and Social Science, 655*(1), 185–208.

Raffaelli, R. (2015). *The re-emergence of an institutional field: Swiss watchmaking.* Cambridge, MA: Harvard Business School.

Redden, E. (2020). Go home? For some students it's not easy. *Inside Higher Ed.* https://www.insidehighered.com/news/2020/03/12/colleges-confronting-coronavirus-tell-students-move-out-many-urge-attention-needs#.XxZGnCCiX0Q.link

Rhoades, G., & Frye, J. (2015). College tuition increases and faculty labor costs: A counterintuitive disconnect [Working Paper]. Center for the Study of Higher Education, University of Arizona.

Rivera, L. (2011). Ivies, extracurriculars, and exclusion: Elite employers' use of educational credentials. *Research in Social Stratification and Mobility, 29*(1), 71–90.

Rivera, L. (2015). *Pedigree: How elite students get elite jobs.* Princeton University Press.

Robertson, S. (2011). Cash cows, backdoor migrants, or activist citizens? International students, citizenship, and rights in Australia. *Ethnic and Racial Studies, 34*(12), 2192–2211.

Robin, S., & Schubert, T. (2013). Cooperation with public research institutions and success in innovation: Evidence from France and Germany. *Research Policy, 42*(1), 149–166.

Rogacheva, Y. (2016). The reception of John Dewey's democratic concept of school in different countries of the world. *Espacio, Tiempo y Educación, 3*(2), 65–87.

Rogers, E. M. (2003). *The diffusion of innovations* (5th ed.). Free Press.

Rosenberg, N. (1994). *Exploring the black box: Technology, economics, and history.* Cambridge University Press.

Rosenberg, N. (2004). *Innovation and economic growth.* OECD. https://www.oecd.org/cfe/tourism/34267902.pdf

Rudolph, F. (1962). *The American college and university: A history.* Vintage Books.

Ryan, C. L., & Bauman, K. (2016). *Educational attainment in the United States: 2015.* U.S. Census Bureau.

Ryan, R. M. (1982). Control and information in the intrapersonal sphere: An extension of cognitive evaluation theory. *Journal of Personality and Social Psychology, 43*(3), 450 461.

Salmi, J. (2009). *The challenge of establishing world-class universities.* World Bank.

Sax, D. (2018). End the innovation obsession. *New York Times.* https://www.nytimes.com/2018/12/07/opinion/sunday/end-the-innovation-obsession.html

Schaefer, R. T. (2012). *Sociology: A brief introduction* (10th ed.). McGraw-Hill.

Schoeman, R. (2016). Why is Germany a powerhouse in research innovation? *Culture Trip.* https://theculturetrip.com/europe/germany/articles/germany-technology-research-and-innovation

Schumpeter, J. A. (1939). *Business cycles: A theoretical, historical, and statistical analysis of the capitalist process* (Vol. 1). McGraw-Hill.

Schumpeter, J. A. (2003). *Capitalism, socialism, and democracy.* Taylor & Francis (Original work published 1942)

Schumpeter, J. A. (2005). Development. *Journal of Economic Literature, 43*(1), 108–120. (Original work published 1932)

Schwab, K. (2018). *The global competitiveness report 2018.* World Economic Forum. http://www3.weforum.org/docs/GCR2018/05FullReport/TheGlobalCompetitivenessReport2018.pdf

Scotchmer, S. (2004). *Innovation and incentives.* MIT Press.

Seligman, A. B. (1997). *The problem of trust.* Princeton University Press.

Seltzer, R. (2018). Moody's: private-college closures at 11 per year. *Inside Higher Ed.* https://www.insidehighered.com/quicktakes/2018/07/25/moodys-private-college-closures-11-year

Seltzer, R. (2020). Housing developer pressured universities on fall plans. *Inside Higher Ed*. https://www.insidehighered.com/news/2020/08/07/housing-developer-reminded-universities-about-project-debt-they-mulled-fall-plans

Shahjahan, R. A., & Hill, R. (2019). Neoliberalism and higher education. In M. David. & M. Amey (Eds.). *Sage encyclopedia of higher education*. Sage.

Shane, S. (2004). *Academic entrepreneurship: University spinoffs and wealth creation*. Northampton, MA: Edward Elgar Publishing.

Shapiro, S. L., Carlson, L. E., Astin, J. A., & Freedman, B. (2006). Mechanisms of mindfulness. *Journal of Clinical Psychology, 62*(3), 373–386.

Shaw, J. S. (2010). Education—A bad public good? *The Independent Review, 15*, 241–256.

Shireman, R. (2017). *The for-profit college story: Scandal, regulate, forget, repeat*. The Century Foundation. https://tcf.org/content/report/profit-college-story-scandal-regulate-forget-repeat/

Shireman, R. (2018a). Federal dollars to for-profit colleges must remain the exception, not the rule. The Century Foundation. https://tcf.org/content/commentary/federal-dollars-profit-colleges-must-remain-exception-not-rule/?agreed=1

Shireman, R. (2018b). We need to retain protections against scam online schools. The Century Foundation. https://tcf.org/content/commentary/need-retain-protections-scam-online-schools/?agreed=1

Shireman, R., & Cochrane, D. (2017). *Encouraging innovation and preventing abuse in for-profit education*. The Century Foundation. https://tcf.org/content/report/encouraging-innovation-preventing-abuses/

Shulman, S., Hopkins, B., Kelchen, R., Persky, J., Yaya, M., Barnshaw, J., & Dunietz, S. J. (2017). Visualizing change: The annual report on the economic status of the profession, 2016–17. *Academe, 103*(2), 4–9.

Sidhu, R. (2009). The "brand name" research university goes global. *Higher Education, 57*(2), 125–140.

Simonton, D. K. (2003). Scientific creativity as constrained stochastic behavior: The integration of product, person, and process perspectives. *Psychological Bulletin, 129*, 475–494.

Sitkin, S., & Roth, N. (1993). Explaining the limited effectiveness of legalistic "remedies" for trust/distrust. *Organization Science, 4*(3), 367–392.

Six, F., & Sorge, A. (2008). Creating a high-trust organization: An exploration into organizational policies that stimulate interpersonal trust building. *Journal of Management Studies, 45*(5), 857–884.

Slaughter, S., & Leslie, L. (1997). *Academic capitalism: Politics, policies, and the entrepreneurial university*. Johns Hopkins University Press.

Slaughter, S., & Rhoades, G. (2004). *Academic capitalism and the new economy: Markets, state, and higher education*. Johns Hopkins University Press.

Smallman, M. (2018). Citizen science and responsible research and innovation. In S. Hecker, M. Haklay, A. Bowser, Z. Makuch, J. Vogel, & A. Boon (Eds.),

Citizen science: Innovation in open science, society, and policy (pp. 241–253). University College London Press.

Sotiris, P. (2014). University movements as laboratories of counter-hegemony. *Journal of Critical Education Policy Studies, 12*(1), 1–21.

Steil, J. P., Albright, L., Rugh, J. S., & Massey, D. S. (2018). The social structure of mortgage discrimination. *Housing Studies, 33*(5), 759–776.

Sternberg, R. J., & Lubart, T. I. (1999). The concept of creativity: Prospects and paradigms. In R. J. Sternberg (Ed.), *Handbook of creativity* (pp. 3–15). Cambridge University Press.

Stilgoe, J., Owen, R., & Macnaghten, P. (2013). Developing a framework for responsible innovation. *Research Policy, 42*(9), 1568–1580.

Strasser, H., & Voswinkel, S. (1997). Confidence in a changing society. In M. K. W. (Ed.), *Interpersonal Trust* (pp. 217–236). Springer.

Stenquist, P. (2021). The future of car navigation has arrived. *New York Times.* https://www.nytimes.com/2021/02/25/business/GPS-car-systems.html

Suspitsyna, T. (2010). Accountability in American education as a rhetoric and a technology of governmentality. *Journal of Education Policy, 25*(5), 567–586.

Takeuchi, H., & Nonaka, I. (1986). The new product development game. *Harvard Business Review, 64*(1), 137–146.

Tang, Y.-Y., Hölzel, B. K., & Posner, M. I. (2015). The neuroscience of mindfulness meditation. *Nature Reviews Neuroscience, 16*, 213–255.

Thorp, H., & Goldstein, B. (2010). *Engines of innovation: The entrepreneurial university in the twenty-first century.* University of North Carolina Press.

Tiedemann, A. (2019). Higher education's future requires entrepreneurial leadership. Babson Thought & Action. https://entrepreneurship.babson.edu/higher-educations-future-requires-entrepreneurial-leadership

Tierney, W. G. (1988). Organizational culture in higher education: Defining the essentials. *Journal of Higher Education, 59*(1), 1–21.

Tierney, W. G. (2006). *Trust and the public good: Examining the cultural conditions of academic work.* Peter Lang.

Tierney, W. G., & Hentschke, G. C. (2007). *New players, different game: Understanding the rise of for-profit colleges and universities.* Johns Hopkins University Press.

Tierney, W. G., & Lanford, M. (2014). The question of academic freedom: Universal right or relative term. *Frontiers of Education in China, 9*(1), 4–23.

Tierney, W. G., & Lanford, M. (2017). Between massification and globalization: Is there a role for global university rankings? In E. Hazelkorn (Ed.), *Global rankings and the geopolitics of higher education* (pp. 295–308). Routledge.

Tierney, W. G., & Lanford, M. (2018). Research in higher education: Cultural perspectives. In J. C. Shin & P. N. Teixeira (Eds.), *Encyclopedia of international higher education systems and institutions* (pp. 1–6). Springer.

Tijssen, R. J. W., & Winnink, J. J. (2018). Capturing "r&d excellence": Indicators, international statistics, and innovative universities. *Scientometrics, 114*(2), 687–699.

Toma, J. D. (2011). *Managing the entrepreneurial university: Legal issues and commercial realities.* Routledge.

Trostel, P. (2015). *It's not just the money: The benefits of college education to individuals and to society.* Lumina Foundation.

Trott, P. (2005). *Innovation management and new product development* (3rd ed.). Pearson.

Trow, M. (1999). Lifelong learning through the new information technologies. *Higher Education Policy, 12*(2), 201–217.

Tsai, W., & Ghoshal, S. (1998). Social capital and value creation: The role of intrafirm networks. *Academy of Management Journal, 41*(4), 464–474.

Tucker, M. (1991). *Ellington: The early years.* University of Illinois Press.

Turan, S. (2000). John Dewey's report of 1924 and his recommendations on the Turkish educational system revisited. *History of Education, 29*(6), 543–555.

Tushman, M. L., & O'Reilly, C. A. (1996). Ambidextrous organizations: Managing evolutionary and revolutionary change. *California Management Review, 38*(4), 8–30.

United National Educational, Social, and Cultural Organization (UNESCO). (2015). *UNESCO Institute of Statistics data on education.* http://data.uis.unesco.org

United States General Accounting Office. (1998). *Technology transfer: Administration of the Bayh-Dole Act by research universities.* U.S. General Accounting Office.

Vaitheeswaran, V. V. (2012). *Need, speed, and greed: How the new rules of innovation can transform business, propel nations to greatness, and tame the world's most wicked problems.* Harper Collins.

Välimaa, J., & Hoffman, D. (2008). Knowledge society discourse and higher education. *Higher Education, 56*(3), 265–285.

van de Leur, W. (2002). *Something to live for: The music of Billy Strayhorn.* Oxford University Press.

Vedder, R. (2012). *Twelve inconvenient truths about American higher education.* Center for College Affordability and Productivity.

Vedder, R. (2017). Seven challenges facing higher education. Forbes. https://www.forbes.com/sites/ccap/2017/08/29/seven-challenges-facing-higher-education

Vedder, R. (2019). *Restoring the promise: Higher education in America.* Independent Institute.

Venegas, K., Cadena, M., Galan, C., Park, E., Astudillo, S., Avilez, A. A., Ward, J. D., Lanford, M., & Tierney, W. G. (2017). *Understanding DACA and the implications for higher education.* Pullias Center for Higher Education, University of Southern California.

Vinsel, L. (2018). Design thinking is a boondoggle. *Chronicle of Higher Education.* https://www.chronicle.com/article/Design-Thinking-Is-a/243472

Verbik, L., & Merkley, C. (2006). *The international branch campus—Models and trends*. Observatory on Borderless Higher Education.

Wadhwa, V. (2013). Peter Thiel promised flying cars; we got caffeine spray instead. *Venture Beat*. https://venturebeat.com/2013/09/11/peter-thiel-promised-flying-cars-instead-we-got-caffeine-spray/

Wang, C. L., & Ahmed, P. K. (2004). Leveraging knowledge in the innovation and learning process at GKN. *International Journal of Technology Management, 27*(6/7), 674–688.

Waters, J. K. (2015, April 16). Disrupting higher education. *Campus Technology*. https://campustechnology.com/articles/2015/04/16/disrupting-higher-education.aspx

Waxman, S. (2012). Against innovation. *Jacobin*. https://jacobinmag.com/2012/09/against-innovation/

Webber, D. A. (2017). State divestment and tuition at public institutions. *Economics of Education Review, 60*, 1–4.

Weick, K. E. (1976). Educational organizations as loosely coupled systems. *Administrative Science Quarterly, 21*(1), 1–19.

Wekullo, C. S. (2017). Outsourcing in higher education: The known and unknown about the practice. *Journal of Higher Education Policy and Management, 39*(4), 453–468.

Wetherbe, J. C. (2013). It's time for tenure to lose tenure. *Harvard Business Review*. https://hbr.org/2013/03/its-time-for-tenure-to-lose-te

Wildavsky, B., Kelly, A. P., & Carey, K. (2011). *Reinventing higher education: The promise of innovation*. Harvard Education Press.

Wike, R., & Stokes, B. (2018). In advanced and emerging economies alike, worries about job automation. Pew Research Center. https://www.pewresearch.org/global/2018/09/13/in-advanced-and-emerging-economies-alike-worries-about-job-automation/

Wilkins, S., & Huisman, J. (2012). The international branch campus as transnational strategy in higher education. *Higher Education, 64*(5), 627–745.

Williams, R. (2020). Dorm operator opposes limits on student occupancy. *Flagpole*. https://flagpole.com/news/news-features/2020/08/12/dorm-operator-opposes-limits-on-student-occupancy/

Woetzel, J., et al. (2016). *People on the move: Global migration's impact and opportunity*. McKinsey Global Institute.

Woideck, C. (1998). *Charlie Parker: His music and life*. University of Michigan Press.

Woodman, R. W., Sawyer, J. E., & Griffin, R. W. (1993). Toward a theory of organizational creativity. *Academy of Management Review, 18*(2), 293–321.

Woodward, M., Hamilton, J., Walton, B., Alberts, G., Fullerton-Smith, S., Day, E., Ringrow, J. (2020). *Electric vehicles: Setting a source for 2030*. Deloitte. https://www2.deloitte.com/us/en/insights/focus/future-of-mobility/electric-vehicle-trends-2030.html

Wölker, A., & Powell, T. E. (2018). Algorithms in the newsroom? News readers' perceived credibility and selection of automated journalism. *Journalism*, *22*(1), 86–103.

Worstall, T. (2011). Baumol's cost disease and the skyrocketing cost of college. *Forbes*. https://www.forbes.com/sites/timworstall/2011/07/10/matt-yglesias-baumols-cost-disease-and-the-skyrocketing-cost-of-college/#2079f4296ddf

Wu, A. M., & Hawkins, J. N. (Eds.). (2018). *Massification of higher education in Asia: Consequences, policy responses, and changing governance.* Springer.

Wu, Y. (2020). Is automated journalistic writing less biased? An experimental test of auto-written and human-written news stories. *Journalism Practice*, *14*(8), 1008–1028.

Yang, R. (2012). Academic entrepreneurialism in a context of altered governance: Some reflections of higher education in Hong Kong. *Globalisation, Societies, and Education*, *10*(3), 387–402.

Zairi, M. (1994). Innovation or innovativeness? Results of a benchmarking study. *Total Quality Management*, *5*(3), 10–16.

Zhao, B. (2018). *Disinvesting in the future? A comprehensive examination of the effects of state appropriations for public higher education.* Federal Reserve Bank of Boston. https://www.bostonfed.org/publications/research-department-working-paper/2018/a-comprehensive-examination-of-the-effects-of-state-appropriations-for-public-higher-education.aspx

Index

CPSIA information can be obtained
at www.ICGtesting.com
Printed in the USA
LVHW021041121122
732942LV00004B/140